D1384777

CROSSCURRENTS *Modern Critiques*

CROSSCURRENTS *Modern Critiques*
Harry T. Moore, *General Editor*

Donald Pizer

Realism and Naturalism

IN NINETEENTH-CENTURY
AMERICAN LITERATURE

WITH A PREFACE BY
Harry T. Moore

Carbondale and Edwardsville

SOUTHERN ILLINOIS UNIVERSITY PRESS

FEFFER & SIMONS, INC.

London and Amsterdam

For Leon Howard

810.4
P695r

FIRST PUBLISHED, FEBRUARY 1966
SECOND PRINTING, MAY 1967

PREFACE

DONALD PIZER, who teaches at Newcomb College of
Tulane University, is one of the leading younger spe-
cialists on fin de siècle American literature. He is the
author of Hamlin Garland's Early Work and Career
(University of California Press, 1960) and the editor
of The Literary Criticism of Frank Norris (University
of Texas Press, 1964). The present book, full of valuable insights and fresh perspectives, is a welcome addition to our knowledge of realism and naturalism in the
American literature of the late nineteenth century.

Mr. Pizer begins with a chapter on realism followed
by one on naturalism, and in each of these he extends
the subject's possibilities. Mr. Pizer views realism, for
example, not in the customary manner; instead of
harping on the limitations of realism, he broadens the
concept to include—in relation to novels of the late
nineteenth century—a subjective element and an ethical idealism. Not content with general assertions, he
clinches his points by useful investigation of three
novels of the period, by Howells, Twain, and James.
In considering naturalism, Mr. Pizer once again gets
away from the time-worn definitions, though accept-
ing them in part: he finds that the naturalistic novels
of the period he is discussing are less "superficial and
reductive" than previous discussions have made them

appear. This time he backs up his assertions with an illuminating exploration of books by Norris, Dreiser, and Stephen Crane.

In succeeding chapters, Mr. Pizer deals not only with other works of the time, but also with the climate of ideas, particularly as represented by literary criticism. Three especially interesting sections are concerned with the application of evolutionary ideas to the literature of the time. Here Mr. Pizer gives particular attention to the too-little-known Thomas Sergeant Perry, who in the 1880's defended realism from an evolutionary (hence radical) point of view. Mr. Pizer shows that, although Perry in his criticism was limited by the age itself, his approach was important because it accepted innovations and was aware of the significance of social forces and comparative studies. Mr. Pizer deals further with Darwinian influences in his chapter on "Howellsian Realism," which treats not only Perry and of course Howells, but also Garland and George Pellew, the last of whom wrote a challenging essay on "The New Battle of the Books" in which he vigorously took up the cause of the new mode of realism. In a third chapter on the influence of evolutionary theory, Mr. Pizer resurrects another critic of the day, William Morton Payne, whose doctrines are also investigated with profit to the reader and to his fuller understanding of the subject. Again finding a "rigid determination" in the outlook of some of these men, Mr. Pizer also once more discovers merits in their attitudes.

The use of such words as explore, find, and discover in relation to his work indicates its value: Mr. Pizer continually offers us fresh views of American writing toward the end of the last century—views which will help us toward a fuller realization of what both earlier and later American literature really mean. Besides the chapters already mentioned, the author includes further material on Norris, both as a critic and as a novelist (in an extended discussion of The Octopus). Stephen Crane's Maggie is also explicated, as well as Howells' The Rise of Silas Lapham; in discussing the latter, Mr. Pizer is particularly good in his treatment of the secondary plot which has vexed so many critics of that novel. And Mr. Pizer provides two excellent chapters on the relationship of Garland and Crane, one on their literary kinship ("The Naturalist as Romantic") and one on their friendship.

It might be added that Mr. Pizer writes smoothly. He has to handle a good deal of factual material, but he never deals with it as if it were overweight stuff. He doesn't attempt any legerdemain in his prose, but it is smooth. This greatly helps the reader as he makes his way through Mr. Pizer's chapters, which clumsy treatment could have made difficult reading. Mr. Pizer has much to say that is significant, and he says it well.

HARRY T. MOORE

Southern Illinois University
September 6, 1965

CONTENTS

INTRODUCTION

THIS BOOK attempts to answer two major questions: how can one best describe realism and naturalism in nineteenth-century American fiction, and what is the relationship between the literary criticism of the age and the emergence and nature of realism and naturalism? The first nine chapters deal more or less directly with these questions. Although the last four chapters of the book are devoted primarily to independent interpretations of particular novels, these interpretations indirectly support the conclusions reached earlier. My method is therefore that of a selective and frequently incomplete examination of particular novels and works of literary criticism. I wish to suggest some of the basic tendencies in late nineteenth-century American fiction and criticism rather than to attempt a description of the period as a whole.

Perhaps I can best summarize my ideas about these tendencies by beginning with the clichés that the literature of the age combined the old and the new and that it looked both backward and forward. The old consisted of a faith in man's worth and freedom, in his power to choose even if he frequently did not choose well. The vestiges of this affirmative view of man's nature and potential are responsible for much of the thematic complexity in late nineteenth-century American fiction. The realists of the seventies and eighties and the naturalists of the nineties reflected in their novels their age's increasing sense of the limitations imposed upon man by his biological past and his social present. But they also persisted—at first confidently and openly, later hesitantly and obliquely—in dramatizing man as a creature of significance and worth. Whether in a Huck Finn beleaguered by a socially corrupted conscience yet possessed of a good heart, or a Carrie grasping for the material plenty of life yet reaching beyond as well, in these and other works the late nineteenth-century American realists and naturalists continued to maintain the tension between actuality and hope which in its various forms has characterized most Western literature since the Renaissance.

The realistic or naturalistic novel is thus not a detached and objective account of the destruction of the individual by material force. Nor are these novels composed of slabs of the commonplace and trivial in experience. Beginning with Twain and James, and continuing more strongly and fully in Norris, Crane, and Dreiser, the novelist depicts life as extraordinary and sensational rather than as placid and commonplace. The first generation of late nineteenth-century novelists dramatized the validity of older faiths in areas of contemporary and local experience recently legitimatized for fictional representation. The increasingly profound involvement of the second generation of novelists in all ranges of life led them to that combination of violent action and degrading detail organized around implicit but oblique systems of value which constitutes the modern tragic vision. Thus, late nineteenth-century fiction is not a long and dull hiatus between the romances of Hawthorne and Melville and those of Faulkner, as much current criticism of American fiction implies. It rather moves toward and eventually embodies the intermingling of the commonplace and the sensational, and of the humanly ennobling and the humanly degrading, which characterizes much of contemporary American fiction.

I have therefore approached late nineteenth-century fiction as though it were something more than the minor details of life sketched in accordance with superficial literary and philosophical formulas. I have been much more summary and boldly analytical in discussing the literary criticism of the age, both because criticism itself is inherently more ideological than fiction and because much of the criticism was argumentative. In general, this criticism—though not as important as either the fiction of the period or the criticism of other periods—is significant because of its role in the rise of realism and because it reflects some of the same tendencies present in fiction. Here is the naive and often dreary application of evolutionary ideas to literature in order to defend or advocate realism. But here also is the continuation in Garland's and Crane's romantic individualism and in Norris's primitivism of a critical subjectivism which stressed above all the truthfulness of an artist's personal vision of life. Here again, therefore, are the outer and inner realities: the crude determinism of impersonal evolutionary law juxtaposed against a faith in a private vision. As in the fiction of the age, these two views do not so much clash as complement each other in a conception of literature and life which is awkwardly complex rather than comfortably obvious.

The large effect of these studies should be to encourage the view that the literature of late nineteenth-century America is not so simple as it sometimes appears to be. The last group of specialized studies confirms this position, for each chapter rejects a conventional simplistic interpretation of a standard novel of the age—that *The Rise of Silas Lapham* is marred by its double plot, that *Maggie* is a superficial study of environmental determinism, and that *The Octopus* can be successfully interpreted by relating its symbols to a cultural myth. (The chapter on the Garland-Crane relationship is outside this intent. It is included because it is often referred to and I wish to make it more generally available.) The tone of many of the studies in this volume is frequently the scholarly and polemical one of certainty and finality. But the impression I really wish to impart is that late nineteenth-century American literature is for the most part unexplored, and that much remains to be done both in the restudy of works buried under older reductive generalizations and in the shaping of new general ideas about the complex patterns of theme and form which emerge out of this and any age's serious attempt to render its values and experience in art.

ii

Except for occasional minor revisions, the text of the chapters is that of their original publication. I have, however, extensively revised the notes in order to bring them up to date and to avoid excessive repetition. The four chapters on evolutionary literary criticism presented a problem because they contain some repetition in the use of supporting quotations and in the discussion of secondary figures. I decided that the material repeated was relatively insignificant and that to remove it without comment or to do so and add elaborate cross references would disturb the coherence and unity of the individual chapters.

I wish to thank the editors of the following journals for permission to republish: *Nineteenth-Century Fiction* ("Late Nineteenth-Century American Realism"); *Bucknell Review* ("Late Nineteenth-Century

American Naturalism"); *Modern Fiction Studies* ("Frank Norris's Definition of Naturalism"); *Philological Quarterly* ("The Evolutionary Foundation of W. D. Howells's *Criticism and Fiction*"); *Texas Studies in Literature and Language* ("Evolution and Criticism: Thomas Sergeant Perry"); *Journal of English and Germanic Philology* ("Evolutionary Criticism and the Defense of Howellsian Realism"); *Journal of Aesthetics and Art Criticism* ("Evolutionary Ideas in Late Nineteenth-Century English and American Literary Criticism"); *American Quarterly* ("Hamlin Garland and Stephen Crane: The Naturalist as Romantic Individualist"); *American Literature* ("The Ethical Unity of *The Rise of Silas Lapham*" and "Synthetic Criticism and Frank Norris's *The Octopus*"); *Huntington Library Quarterly* ("The Garland-Crane Relationship"); and *Criticism* ("Stephen Crane's *Maggie* and American Naturalism"). I also wish to thank the University of Texas Press for permission to republish paragraphs which appeared originally in my edition of *The Literary Criticism of Frank Norris* ("The Significance of Frank Norris's Literary Criticism").

Tulane University   **DONALD PIZER**
August, 1965

Realism and Naturalism

IN NINETEENTH-CENTURY
AMERICAN LITERATURE

1 LATE NINETEENTH-CENTURY AMERICAN REALISM

CRITICS AND LITERARY HISTORIANS of all persuasions have found that such broad descriptive terms as classicism, romanticism, and realism are valuable and necessary despite their multiple meanings. To describe a writer, work, theme, or genre as classic, romantic, or realistic is to employ a useful frame of reference whence further examination and discussion may proceed. What is required, of course, is some general agreement on the frame of reference, and for the past several decades there have been frequent attempts to sharpen our awareness of the full implications of the terms classicism and romanticism. Realism, as a more recent, seemingly less complicated literary mode, has had less such attention devoted to it. Indeed, George J. Becker's essay in *Modern Language Quarterly* over fifteen years ago has been one of the few notable attempts to define realism.[1] Becker, basing his definition upon European and American fiction since approximately 1870, listed three criteria of the realistic mode. The first is verisimilitude of detail derived from observation and documentation. The second is an effort to approach the norm of experience—that is, a reliance upon the representative rather than the exceptional in plot, setting, and character. The last is an objective, so far as an artist can achieve objectivity, rather than a subjective or idealistic view of human nature and experience.[2]

It would be difficult to quarrel with Becker's definition, given the wide range of his survey. His definition clearly requires modification, however, if it is to be applicable within narrower national and chronological limits, and such a modification is particularly important in American literary history, where realism is used to characterize an entire age. What I propose to do, then, is to use Becker's criteria of verisimilitude, representativeness, and objectivity as a means of approaching a definition of realism as it actually functioned in the late nineteenth-century American novel. My belief is that late nineteenth-century American realism varies from Becker's definition in two important ways. First, it achieves a greater diversity in subject matter than is suggested by the criterion of the representative. Secondly, it is essentially subjective and idealistic in its view of human nature and experience—that is, it is ethically idealistic. Three texts will illustrate my thesis: William Dean Howells's *The Rise of Silas Lapham* (1885), Mark Twain's *Adventures of Huckleberry Finn* (1884), and Henry James's *What Maisie Knew* (1897). I realize, of course, that earlier or later works by these novelists may or may not support my belief, and that works by other contemporaneous authors may contradict it as well. I am also aware that the realism of the nineties was in many respects less optimistic than that of the seventies. But the three works chosen are characteristic and well-known novels by the three leading realists of the period, and a generalization drawn from them need not be universally applicable to have implications for the period as a whole.

The three works are novels of manners in the sense that each focuses on the relationship of its central character to a particular social world. Each introduces a moral tension or conflict between the protagonist and his milieu. *The Rise of Silas Lapham* centers on the individual's relation to the business world; *Huck Finn* on his relation to the world of formalized codes of social belief and behavior; *What Maisie Knew* to the world of extramarital sexual intrigue.

The Rise of Silas Lapham clearly fulfills the initial two criteria of Becker's definition. Indeed, it is offered as a prime example of realistic fiction by Gordon Haight in his essay on Howells in the *Literary History of the United States* and by M. H. Abrams in his definition of realism in *A Glossary of Literary Terms*. The world of Silas Lapham is that of commonplace late nineteenth-century Boston. Here is no Ahab pursuing his whale with monomaniacal frenzy, no Leatherstocking matching wits and skill with red or white foes in the forest, no Chillingworth brewing potions, but Lapham going down to business each day, taking pride in his family, his trotter, his success in the world. That world, however, is not free from evil, and the moral drama in which Ahab, Leatherstocking, and Chillingworth played is still on the boards. But now, in everyday Boston, evil is more commonplace, is more that which we are accustomed to in our everyday affairs, is more realistic, if you will. It is the falsifications of Silas's former business partner; it is the willingness of the English agents to defraud their backers; it is Silas's own hardhearted treatment of his partner earlier in their careers. Moreover, evil is now so prevalent that the individual immersed in it is frequently unaware that he is participating in or committing evil. The point of the novel, however, is that Silas, though years of business life have partially atrophied his moral sense, does, at a moment of crisis, realize that a particular action is evil and does have the moral strength to make the correct choice. In his rejection of the opportunity to save his fortune, he rises not only above his earlier moral muteness, but also (and more importantly) above the society around him. He is ultimately morally superior to the business world which is his world.

Of course, Howells advocated probability of motive, and Silas's moral values do not appear from nowhere. They are founded in his poor but honest Vermont boyhood and in his wife's conscience. But explaining the source of an action does not make that action probable. Howells's belief in Silas's ability to rise above his world is basically idealistic, since it is a private belief in what should be rather than a depiction of what usually is. While Howells's conception of man and society is not crudely primitivistic, it owes much to a belief in the individual's innate moral sense and in the corrupting effects of the pressures of society. Such a belief does not have to be set in a jungle or forest to be operative.

Adventures of Huckleberry Finn, like much of Twain's work, is in the local color and tall tale traditions. From both of these Twain derived an emphasis on verisimilitude of detail. In *Huck Finn*, Twain's introductory note on accents is an indication of his conscious attempt to achieve accurate detail. But though Tom and Huck and Jim may be representative characters, their adventures are picaresque and are unusual rather than commonplace. We sometimes forget that the plot of the novel encompasses a full range of acts of violence, from the ambuscade of the A-rabs to the near-lynching of Jim. It is possible, however, to struggle with the idea that the total effect of *Huck Finn* is realistic despite the extraordinary nature of Huck's adventures. This effect is partially gained by the satiric thrust of the novel, by its constant puncturing of the falsely heroic and the sentimental, by its burlesque of the extraordinary rather than its literal acceptance of it. In addition, *Huck Finn* is somewhat like *Tom Jones* in that the intense verisimilitude of detail in the portrayal of individual incidents and characters dominates the novel and tends to blur the exceptional quality of the incidents themselves. In short, part of Twain's purpose in his use of the extraordinary is to deflate it, and his use of vividly concrete detail helps achieve this end. In any case, though Twain does not completely fulfill the criterion of the representative, he nevertheless in his own way justifies his traditional inclusion among the realists.

In *Huck Finn*, as in *The Rise of Silas Lapham*, the social world is the embodiment of evil. Twain's world is larger than Howells's, however, and includes many forms of codified and institutionalized behavior and belief. Huck's decision not to inform on Jim (in the chapter "You Can't Pray a Lie") reveals the power of such codes. His resolution, Huck decides, is wrong and will result in his damnation. The irony, of course, is that he is led to this conclusion by what he knows is right—the code of slavery—although he does what he is instinctively led to do. Like Howells, then, Twain indicated that the world around us is frequently corrupt and false. This belief, which received its most obvious fictional representation in Huck's crisis, is also apparent in several other major incidents in the novel and in its very structure. Tom's romantic code of behavior, the code of the feud, of honor, of the mob, all are shown to lead to tragedy or near-tragedy—to the true damnation of the participant. Huck and Jim, drifting down the Mississippi, seek to evade these codes.

As Howells had done, Twain revealed his faith in man's ability to rise above the evil around him and achieve an ethical victory. Huck's moral values, like those of Silas, are effectively anticipated, since he has come to know and to value Jim as a companion in escape and as a human being. But Huck's ability to make the correct moral choice despite the world around him is both more brilliantly ironic and more fundamentally idealistic than Silas's. Silas at least knew what was right and what was wrong. Huck must struggle against a false knowledge of right and wrong, and his correct decision is indicative of Twain's faith in the individual's ability to rise above society even when he is unaware that he is so doing.

What Maisie Knew is a psychological novel. James's interest, as he tells in his preface, was not primarily in the story, but rather in its refraction through the intelligence of a child. This technique would both illumine her mind and—because of her youth and freshness of vision—cast an ironic glow over the sordidness of the story. In order to achieve this end, James informs us, verisimilitude required that the child be a female rather than "a rude little boy." In addition, in order for the child to be the major source of moral insight, as well as "ironic center," she would have to be invested with "perceptions easily and almost infinitely quickened" and great "vivacity of intelligence," though not "in a manner too grossly to affront intelligence." James's intent was to present experience through a consciousness that had the ability to absorb and contemplate experience and ultimately the ability to draw moral deductions from that process. The need for such a consciousness, it is clear, encouraged the choice of an unusual central intelligence, one exceptional in perception and sensitivity, and therefore beyond the range of the representative. Yet though the intelligence itself is unusual, verisimilitude and probability are maintained as guides in the presentation of the refractor, and the total effect is that of psychological realism. In other

words, James's practice of the psychological novel
inherently encouraged a violation of one of the criteria
of realism while at the same time he attempted to
achieve the effect of realism.

As Twain does in *Huck Finn,* James juxtaposes a
child and an evil world. The various adults who constitute Maisie's world shuttle her among themselves either to vex one another or to provide a screen for illicit
relations. By the close of the novel Maisie knows two
things. She has a knowledge of the world of adult
promiscuity, jealousy, and desire. She has also, however, discovered her moral sense, partially under the
guidance of Mrs. Wix, but (as becomes apparent
when Mrs. Wix herself almost succumbs at the close)
more as a reaction against the world around her. It is as
if the irritation of that world had caused her moral
sense to emerge and at last to assert itself in her refusal
to remain with Sir Claude, whom she loves, under
circumstances which she recognizes as both absolutely
and pragmatically evil. Maisie, too, then, has risen
above the world and has achieved an arduous moral
victory. Huck's victory was difficult because it required
him to subvert the dictates of knowledge and conscience. Silas's victory required the sacrifice of riches,
Maisie's of love. But for all three victory can be and is
gained.

Howells, Twain, and James indicate the ideal possibilities of action within particular social contexts,
rather than the way most men act within these contexts. Those who are willing to struggle against the
general current, and to be damned or to sacrifice
wealth and love in the name of principle, have been
and still are the exception, not the rule. The three
writers, in short, dramatize a vision of experience in
which individuals achieve that which is still a goal for
mankind at large. This view of experience is, of course,

a traditional one of much humanistic art, as well as a product of the more masculine side of nineteenth-century American romantic idealism—the side that does not minimize the strength of the forces tending to corrupt the spirit of man while it continues to affirm both the necessary and probable victory of the human spirit over these forces. The three writers gain much of their thematic power from their adherence to this view of experience. It is not a view, however, which fulfills the criterion of realism requiring an objective rather than a subjective or idealistic vision of human nature and experience.

Moreover, two of the three writers extend the subject matter of realism beyond the representative. Howells alone fulfills this criterion, and is a kind of mean in this respect, whereas Twain devotes much of his attention to the unusual in incident, James to the unusual in character. The significance of this extension is that Twain and James, rather than Howells, indicate the direction American fiction was to take. For although very few twentieth-century novelists have been concerned with the commonplace, many of our major writers have been occupied with what it is possible to call the horizontal and vertical extensions of realism—that is, the fiction of external violence and interior monologue.

Late nineteenth-century American realism was attacked in its own time for unidealized pictures of commonplace life, and for many years continued to be so characterized; in fact, however, it was neither unidealized nor—for the most part—commonplace. Rather, in its variation from these two criteria of a conventional definition of realism—that is, in its ethical idealism and in its exploration of richly diverse experience—it achieved both its vitality and its promise of future growth.

MOST LITERARY CRITICS and historians who attempt
definitions are aware of the dangers and advantages
inherent in this enterprise. But few, I believe, recognize that many literary genres and modes have their
barriers of established terms and ideas to overcome or
outflank. The writer who seeks to define tragedy
usually finds that his definition takes shape around
such traditional guideposts as the tragic hero, the
tragic flaw, recognition and catharsis, and so on. American naturalism, as a concept, has two such channelled
approaches to its definition. The first is that since
naturalism comes after realism, and since it seems to
take literature in the same direction as realism, it is
primarily an "extension" or continuation of realism—
only a little different. The second almost inevitable
approach involves this difference. The major distinction between realism and naturalism, most critics
agree, is the particular philosophical orientation of
the naturalists. A traditional and widely accepted
concept of American naturalism, therefore, is that it is
essentially realism infused with a pessimistic determinism. Richard Chase argues that American naturalism is
realism with a "necessitarian ideology," and George J.
Becker (defining all naturalism, including American)
considers it as "no more than an emphatic and explicit

philosophical position taken by some realists," the position being a "pessimistic materialistic determinism." [1] The common belief is that the naturalists were like the realists in their fidelity to the details of contemporary life, but that they depicted everyday life with a greater sense of the role of such causal forces as heredity and environment in determining behavior and belief.

This traditional approach to naturalism through realism and through philosophical determinism is historically justifiable and has served a useful purpose, but it has also handicapped thinking both about the movement as a whole and about individual works within the movement. It has resulted in much condescension toward those writers who are supposed to be naturalists yet whose fictional sensationalism (an aspect of romanticism) and moral ambiguity (a quality inconsistent with the absolutes of determinism) appear to make their work flawed specimens of the mode.

I would like, therefore, to propose a modified definition of late nineteenth-century American naturalism.[2] For the time being, let this be a working definition, to be amplified and made more concrete by the illustrations from which it has been drawn. I suggest that the naturalistic novel usually contains two tensions or contradictions, and that the two in conjunction comprise both an interpretation of experience and a particular aesthetic recreation of experience. In other words, the two constitute the theme and form of the naturalistic novel. The first tension is that between the subject matter of the naturalistic novel and the concept of man which emerges from this subject matter. The naturalist populates his novel primarily from the lower middle class or the lower class. His characters are the poor, the uneducated, the unsophisticated. His fictional world is that of the commonplace and unheroic in which life would seem to be chiefly the dull round of daily existence, as we ourselves usually conceive of our lives. But the naturalist discovers in this world those qualities of man usually associated with the heroic or adventurous, such as acts of violence and passion which involve sexual adventure or bodily strength and which culminate in desperate moments and violent death. A naturalistic novel is thus an extension of realism only in the sense that both modes often deal with the local and contemporary. The naturalist, however, discovers in this material the extraordinary and excessive in human nature.

The second tension involves the theme of the naturalistic novel. The naturalist often describes his characters as though they are conditioned and controlled by environment, heredity, instinct, or chance. But he also suggests a compensating humanistic value in his characters or their fates which affirms the significance of the individual and of his life. The tension here is that between the naturalist's desire to represent in fiction the new, discomforting truths which he has found in the ideas and life of his late nineteenth-century world, and also his desire to find some meaning in experience which reasserts the validity of the human enterprise. The naturalist appears to say that although the individual may be a cipher in a world made amoral by man's lack of responsibility for his fate, the imagination refuses to accept this formula as the total meaning of life and so seeks a new basis for man's sense of his own dignity and importance.

The naturalistic novel is therefore not so superficial or reductive as it implicitly appears to be in its conventional definition. It involves a belief that life on its lowest levels is not so simple as it seems to be from higher levels. It suggests that even the least significant human being can feel and strive powerfully and can suffer the extraordinary consequences of his emotions, and that no range of human experience is free of the moral complexities and ambiguities which Milton set his fallen angels to debating.³ Naturalism reflects an affirmative ethical conception of life, for it asserts the value of all life by endowing the lowest character with emotion and defeat and with moral ambiguity, no matter how poor or ignoble he may seem. The naturalistic novel derives much of its aesthetic effect from these contrasts. It involves us in the experience of a life both commonplace and extraordinary, both familiar and strange, both simple and complex. It pleases us with its sensationalism without affronting our sense of probability. It discovers the "romance of the commonplace," as Frank Norris put it. Thus, the melodramatic sensationalism and moral "confusion" which are often attacked in the naturalistic novel should really be incorporated into a normative definition of the mode and be recognized as its essential constituents.

The three novels which I have chosen to illustrate this definition, and also to suggest the possible range of variation within it, are Frank Norris's *McTeague* (1899), Theodore Dreiser's *Sister Carrie* (1900), and Stephen Crane's *The Red Badge of Courage* (1895). These works are important novels by the three leading late nineteenth-century American naturalists, and each novel has frequently been read as a key example of its author's values and his fictional form. A definition drawn from these three novels will not be applicable to all late nineteenth-century naturalistic fiction. But, given the significance of these writers and of these novels, it would, I believe, be a useful introduction to this major movement in American literary history.

ii

A good deal of *McTeague* is devoted to depicting the routine, ordered world of Polk Street, the lower middle class service street in San Francisco on which McTeague practices and lives. The life of Polk Street enters the novel in two ways—through set pieces describing street activities or the daily lives of the central characters in relation to the life of the street, and through constant incidental allusion to its activities and inhabitants. Norris dramatically establishes Polk Street as above all a life of the repetitious and constant. The street exists as a source of the ordered and the routine in McTeague's life, as a world where the harness shop, the grocery, and the car conductors' coffee joint are always available in their set roles, where the children go to school at the same time each day, followed by the shop clerks coming to work, and so on. McTeague is settled and content in this life, and we recognize that his inner needs and outer world are in harmony.

A central theme in Norris's work is that beneath the surface of our placid, everyday lives there is turbulence, that the romance of the extraordinary is not limited to the distant in time and place but can be found "in the brownstone house on the corner and in the office building downtown." [4] Norris therefore used the incident which had stimulated him to write the novel, a vicious murder in a San Francisco kindergarten, as a controlling paradox in *McTeague* as in scene after scene he introduces the sensational into the commonplace activities and setting of Polk Street. So we have such incidents as McTeague grossly kissing the anesthetized Trina in his dental parlor, or the nearly murderous fight between Marcus and McTeague at the picnic. Some of the best moments in the novel powerfully unite these two streams of the commonplace and the extraordinary. In one such moment the frightened and incoherent Trina, having just found Maria's corpse with its cut throat and its blood soaked clothes, rushes out into the everyday routine of Polk

Street and has difficulty convincing the butcher's boy that something is wrong or even convincing herself that it is not improper "to make a disturbance and create a scene in the street." [5]

Norris believed that the source of this violence beneath the surface placidity of life is the presence in all men of animal qualities which have played a major role in man's evolutionary development but which are now frequently atavistic and destructive.[6] Norris's theme is that man's racial atavism (particularly his brute sexual desires) and man's individual family heritage (alcoholic degeneracy in McTeague's case) can combine as a force toward reversion, toward a return to the emotions and instincts of man's animal past. McTeague is in one sense a "special case" of reversion, since his atavistic brutality is in part caused by his degenerate parents. He is also, however, any man caught up in the net of sex, and in this second aspect of man's inherited animal nature Norris introduces a tragic element into McTeague's fall, an element which contributes to the novel's thematic tension.

In describing the courtship of Trina and McTeague, Norris is at pains to stress their overt sexual innocence yet intuitive sexuality. The woman in Trina "was not yet awakened; she was yet, as one might say, without sex." [20] For McTeague, Trina is his "first experience. With her the feminine element suddenly entered his little world. It was not only her that he saw and felt, it was the woman, the whole sex, an entire new humanity . . . ." [23] Despite their innocence and lack of experience, both react intuitively and atavistically— McTeague desiring to seize and possess her, she instinctively withdrawing yet desiring to be conquered.

The most important sexual encounter between McTeague and Trina occurs at the B Street Station where McTeague for a second time proposes. When

Trina hesitates, he seizes her "in his enormous arms, crushing down her struggle with his immense strength. Then Trina gave up, all in an instant, turning her head to his. They kissed each other, grossly, full in the mouth." [72] Within the literary conventions of the day, this kiss symbolizes Trina's sexual submission. At this moment the strands in the web of sexual determinism begin the pull taut, for "the instant she allowed him to kiss her, he thought less of her. She was not so desirable, after all." [73] McTeague senses this diminution along with a dim awareness "that this must be so, that it belonged to the changeless order of things—the man desiring the woman only for what she withholds; the woman worshipping the man for that which she yields up to him. With each concession gained the man's desire cools; with every surrender made the woman's adoration increases." [73] Norris is concerned in this second meeting not with a special flaw in McTeague or Trina but with a sexual determinism affecting all men. The possessive sexual desire of the man aroused by the first woman he experiences sensually, the instinctive desire of the woman for sexual submission responding to the first man who assaults her—these are the atavistic animal forces which bring Trina and McTeague together.

A major theme in *McTeague* is therefore that of the sexual tragedy of man and woman. Caught up by drives and instincts beyond their control or comprehension, they mate by chance. In *McTeague* sex is that which comes to all men and women, disrupting their lives and placing them in relationships which the sanctity of marriage cannot prevent from ending in chaos and destruction. Norris does not tell the old tale of the fallen fornicator, as he does in *Vandover and the Brute*, but rather reaches out toward the unexplored ground of the human dilemma of sexual attraction.

The tension between this deterministic aspect of *McTeague* and its humanistic element does not lie in McTeague as a fully developed tragic figure. Rather, it is contained in the theme that man can seldom escape the violence inherent in his own nature, that man's attempt to achieve an ordered world is constantly thwarted by man himself. Norris devotes much attention to the element of order in the details of McTeague's life not only because of his belief in the romance of the commonplace but because the destruction of that order is the source of the tragic quality in McTeague's fall and of our own compassionate involvement with him despite his grotesqueness. Norris carefully documents McTeague's life as a dentist and as an inhabitant of Polk Street because the habitual tasks and minor successes of this life represent the order and stability which McTeague requires. In the course of the novel we begin to feel compassion for him as he becomes a victim of Trina's avarice and as we recognize that his emerging brutality is at least partly the result of the destruction of his world. When McTeague learns that he can no longer practice dentistry, his reaction is that of a man whose life is emptied of all meaning. In a scene of considerable power Trina comes upon him sitting in his dental chair, "looking stupidly out of the window, across the roofs opposite, with an unseeing gaze, his red hands lying idly in his lap." [229] We are never completely one with McTeague; his brute strength and dull mind put us off. But because he is trapped in the universal net of sex, and because we recognize the poignancy of the loss of his world, we respond to him ultimately as a human being in distress, as a figure of some significance despite his limitations—as a man, in short, whose fall contains elements of the tragic.

For *McTeague* is in part a tragic novel. True,

McTeague neither bears full responsibility for his fate nor is he in any sense noble or profound. He is rather like Gervaise in *L'Assommoir:* they are both poor creatures who want above all a place to rest and be content, yet who are brought low by their needs and desires. There is a sense of common humanity in McTeague's fall, and that quality is perhaps the modern residue of the tragic theme, since we are no longer certain of man's transcendent nobility or of the reality of major responsibility for our fates. The theme of *McTeague* is not that drunkenness leads to a tragic fall, but that tragedy is inherent in the human situation given man's animal past and the possibility that he will be dominated by that past in particular circumstances. Norris does not deny the strength of man's past or present animality, but neither does he deny the poignancy of the fall of even such a gross symbol of this animality as McTeague. It is out of this tension that much of the meaning and power of the novel arises.

iii

Even more than Norris, Theodore Dreiser creates a sense of the solidity of life. His early novels in particular affirm that we cannot escape the impact of physical reality and that this fact is one of the few that man may know with certainty. So the several worlds of Carrie—her sister's working class existence, her life with Drouet in Chicago and with Hurstwood in New York—achieve a sense of massiveness both in their painstaking documentation and in their inescapable effect on Carrie. The effect on us, however, is not only to enforce a sense of the importance of clothes, of furniture, of how much one owes the grocer and of exactly how much one earns and spends—the impact, too, is of normalcy, of the steady pace of life, since life does indeed seem to be measured out in coffee spoons. Dreiser's ability to capture the tangible commonplace of everyday existence powerfully suggests that the commonplace and everyday are the essence of experience, particularly since he returns again and again to the unexciting details of the furnishings of an apartment or the contents of a meal. Moreover, Dreiser's dispassionate tone contributes to this effect. He is, indeed, something of an ironist. He frequently sets events or beliefs in ironic juxtaposition, as when Carrie is worried that Hurstwood will discover that she and Drouet are unmarried though she herself is unaware that Hurstwood *is* married. But Dreiser's irony differs from Crane's intense and pervasive ironic vision of life, a vision which colors every incident or observation in Crane's work with the implication that things are not what they seem. Dreiser's plodding, graceless paragraphs imply the opposite—that the concrete world he so seriously details is real and discernible and that nothing can shake or undermine it.

Dreiser's central theme in *Sister Carrie*, however, sets forth the idea—Lionel Trilling to the contrary [7]—that the physically real is not the only reality and that men seek something in life beyond it. His theme is that those of a finer, more intense, more emotional nature who desire to break out of their normal solid world—whether it be a Carrie oppressed by the dull repetitiousness and crudity of her sister's home, or a Hurstwood jaded by the middle class trivialities of his family—that when such as these strive to discover a life approximate to their natures they introduce into their lives the violent and the extraordinary. Carrie leaves her sister's flat for two illicit alliances, attracted to each man principally by the opportunities he offers for a better life. Drouet and Hurstwood represent to her not so much wealth or sexual attraction as an appeal to something intangibly richer and fuller in herself. She is drawn to each in turn, and then finally to Ames, because each appeals to some quality in her temperament which she finds unfulfilled in her life of the moment. Dreiser's depiction of her almost asexual relations with all of these men represents less his capitulation to contemporary publishing restrictions (although some of this is present) than his desire that the three characters reflect the upward course of Carrie's discovery and realization of her inner nature. Finally, Carrie's career on the stage symbolizes both the emotional intensity she is capable of bringing to life and the fact that she requires the intrinsically extraordinary and exciting world of the theatre to call forth and embody her emotional depth.

Hurstwood also introduces the sensational into his life by reaching out beyond his established world. For him, the extraordinary arises from his attempt to gain and then hold Carrie, since she represents to him his last opportunity to grasp life fully and intensely. We follow him as he breaks the seemingly set mold of his life by his theft and by his elopement. His participation in the violence of the street car strike is his final attempt to recover his fortunes (and Carrie) in New York. With Carrie gone, he sinks still further and eventually commits suicide.

Hurstwood's suicide can be explored as a typical example of Dreiser's combination of the concretely commonplace and the sensational. It takes place in a cheap Bowery hotel. Hurstwood's method is to turn on the gas, not resolutely but hesitantly, and then to say weakly, " 'What's the use?' " as he "stretched himself to rest." [8] Dreiser thus submerges an inherently sensational event in the trivial and unemotional. He not only "takes the edge off" the extraordinariness of the event by his full and detached elaboration of its commonplace setting but also casts it in the imagery of enervation and rest. This scene is in one sense a special instance, since Hurstwood seeks death as a refuge. But Dreiser's total effect as a novelist is often similar to the effect produced by this scene as he dramatizes throughout *Sister Carrie* the solidity and therefore seeming normalcy of experience and yet its underlying extraordinariness if man seeks beyond the routine. His principal aesthetic impact, however, is different from that of Norris, who appears to combine the sensational and commonplace much as Dreiser does. Norris's effect is basically that of dramatic sensationalism, of the excitement of violence and sudden death. Dreiser's effect is more thematic and less scenic because he colors the sensational with the same emotional stolidity with which he characterizes all experience. It is not only that the sensational and extraordinary exist in our commonplace lives, Dreiser appears to say, but that they are so pervasive and implicit in our experience that their very texture differs little from the ordinary course of events. Thus, such potentially exciting and dramatically sensational moments in Dreiser's fiction as the seduction of Jennie Gerhardt or the imprisonment of Frank Cowperwood have an almost listless dullness compared to Norris's treatment of parallel events in his fiction.

Carrie, like many of Dreiser's characters, has her life shaped by chance and need. Chance involves her with Drouet and later plays a large role in Hurstwood's theft and therefore in her own departure with him. Her needs are of two kinds—first to attain the tangible objects and social symbols of comfort and beauty which she sees all around her in Chicago and New York, and then to be loved. Of the major forces in her life, it is primarily her desire for objects that furnish a sense of physical and mental well-being—for fine cloth-

ing and furniture and attractive apartments and satisfactory food—which determines much of her life. As
she gains more of these, her fear of returning to
poverty and crudity—to her sister's condition—impels
her to seek even more vigorously. Much of the concrete
world that Dreiser fills in so exhaustively in *Sister
Carrie* thus exists as a determining force in Carrie's
life, first moving her to escape it, as in her encounters
with working-class Chicago, and then to reach out for
it, as when Drouet takes her to a good restaurant and
buys her some fashionable clothes and so introduces
into her imagination the possibility of making these a
part of her life.

But Carrie's response to her needs is only one side of
her nature. She also possesses a quality which is intrinsic to her being, though its external shape (a Drouet, a
dress seen on the street) is determined by accidental
circumstance. For in this his first novel Dreiser endows
Carrie with the same capacity to wonder and to dream
which he felt so strongly in himself. It is this ability to
dream about the nature of oneself and one's fate and
of where one is going and how one will get there and to
wonder whether happiness is real and possible or only
an illusion—it is this capacity which ultimately questions the reality and meaning of the seemingly solid
and plain world in which we find ourselves.

This "dream" quality underlies the most striking
symbol in the novel, the rocking chair. Occasionally
the rocking chair has been interpreted as principally a
symbol of circularity because Carrie rocks on her first
night in Chicago and again at the novel's close in her
New York apartment.[9] It is suggested that Dreiser
means to imply that nothing really has happened to
Carrie, that although her outer circumstances have
changed, she is essentially the same both morally and
spiritually. The symbol does indeed function partly in

this way, but its primary emphasis is not the negative one of nothing changed and therefore nothing gained or learned. Its stress is rather the positive idea that Carrie continues to have the ability to wonder about herself and her future, that her imaginative response to life has not been dulled by experience. Although she has not achieved the happiness that she thought accompanied the life she desired and which she now has, she will continue to search. Perhaps Ames represents the next, higher step in this quest, Dreiser implies. But in any case, she possesses this inner force, a force which is essentially bold and free. Although it brings her worry and loneliness—the rocking chair symbolizes these as well—it is an element in her which Dreiser finds estimable and moving. She will always be the dreamer, Dreiser says, and though her dreams take an earthly shape controlled by her world, and though she is judged immoral by the world because she violates its conventions in pursuit of her dreams, she has for Dreiser—and for us, I believe—meaning and significance and stature because of her capacity to rock and dream, to question life and to pursue it. Thus Carrie seeks to fulfill each new venture and gain each new object as though these were the only realities of life, and yet by her very dissatisfaction and questioning of what she has gained to imply the greater reality of the mind and spirit that dreams and wonders. The rocking chair goes nowhere, but it moves, and in that paradox lies Dreiser's involvement with Carrie and his ability to communicate the intensity and nature of her quest. For in his mind, too, the world is both solid and unknowable, and man is ever pursuing and never finding.

iv

The Red Badge of Courage also embodies a different combination of the sensational and commonplace than that found in *McTeague*. Whereas Norris demonstrates that the violent and the extraordinary are present in seemingly dull and commonplace lives, Crane, even more than Dreiser, is intent on revealing the commonplace nature of the seemingly exceptional. In *The Red Badge* Henry Fleming is a raw, untried country youth who seeks the romance and glory of war but who finds that his romantic, chivalric preconceptions of battle are false. Soldiers and generals do not strike heroic poses; the dead are not borne home triumphantly on their shields but fester where they have fallen; and courage is not a conscious striving for an ideal mode of behavior but a temporary delirium derived from animal fury and social pride or fear. A wounded officer worries about the cleanliness of his uniform; a soldier sweats and labors at his arms "like a laborer in a foundry";[10] and mere chance determines rewards and punishments—the death of a Conklin, the red badge of a Fleming. War to Crane is like life itself in its injustice, in its mixing of the ludicrous and the momentarily exhilarating, in its self-deceptions, and in its acceptance of appearances for realities. Much of Crane's imagery in the novel is therefore consciously and pointedly antiheroic, not only in his obviously satirical use of conventional chivalric imagery in unheroic situations (a soldier bearing a rumor comes "waving his [shirt] banner-like" and adopting "the important air of a herald in red and gold" [238]) but also more subtly in his use of machine and animal imagery to deflate potentially heroic moments.

Crane's desire to devalue the heroic in war stems in part from his stance as an ironist reacting against a literary and cultural tradition of idealized courage and chivalry. But another major element in his desire to reduce war to the commonplace arises from his casting of Fleming's experiences in the form of a "life" or initiation allegory. Henry Fleming is the universal youth who leaves home unaware of himself or the world. His participation in battle is his introduction to life as for the first time he tests himself and his preconceptions of experience against experience itself. He emerges at the end of the battle not entirely self-perceptive or firm-willed—Crane is too much the ironist for such a reversal—but rather as one who has encountered some of the strengths and some of the failings of himself and others. Crane implies that although Fleming may again run from battle and although he will no doubt always have the human capacity to rationalize his weaknesses, he is at least no longer the innocent.

If *The Red Badge* is viewed in this way—that is, as an antiheroic allegory of "life"—it becomes clear that Crane is representing in his own fashion the naturalistic belief in the interpenetration of the commonplace and the sensational. All life, Crane appears to be saying, is a struggle, a constant sea of violence in which we inevitably immerse ourselves and in which we test our beliefs and our values. War is an appropriate allegorical symbol of this test, for to Crane violence is the very essence of life, not in the broad Darwinian sense of a struggle for existence or the survival of the fittest, but rather in the sense that the proving and testing of oneself, conceived both realistically and symbolically, entails the violent and the deeply emotional, that the finding of oneself occurs best in moments of stress and is itself often an act of violence. To Crane, therefore, war as an allegorical setting for the emergence of youth into knowledge embodies both the violence of this birth and the commonplaces of life which the birth reveals—that men are controlled by the trivial, the accidental, the degradingly unheroic, despite the preservation of such accoutrements of the noble as a red badge or a captured flag. Crane shows us what Norris and Dreiser only suggest, that there is no separation between the sensational and the commonplace, that the two are coexistent in every aspect and range of life. He differs from Norris in kind and from Dreiser in degree in that his essentially ironic imagination leads him to reverse the expected and to find the commonplace in the violent rather than the sensational beneath the trivial. His image of life as an unheroic battle captures in one ironic symbol both his romanticism and his naturalism—or, in less literary terms, his belief that we reveal character in violence but that human character is predominantly fallible and self-deceptive.

Much of Crane's best fiction displays this technique of ironic deflation. In *Maggie,* a young urchin defends the honor of Rum Alley on a heap of gravel; in "The Open Boat," the stalwart oiler suffers an inconsequential and meaningless death; in "The Blue Hotel," the death of the Swede is accompanied by a derisive sign on the cash register; and in "The Bride Comes to Yellow Sky," the long-awaited "chivalric" encounter is thwarted by the bride's appearance. Each of these crucial or significant events has at its core Crane's desire to reduce the violent and extraordinary to the commonplace, a reduction which indicates both his ironic vision of man's romantic pretensions and his belief in the reality of the fusion of the violent and the commonplace in experience.

As was true of Norris and Dreiser, Crane's particular way of combining the sensational and the commonplace is closely related to the second major aspect of his naturalism, the thematic tension or complexity he embodies in his work. *The Red Badge* presents a vision of man as a creature capable of advancing in some areas of knowledge and power but forever imprisoned within the walls of certain inescapable human and social limitations. Crane depicts the similarity between Henry Fleming's "will" and an animal's instinctive response to crisis or danger. He also presents Fleming's discovery that he is enclosed in a "moving box" of "tradition and law" [259] even at those moments when he believes himself capable of rational decision and action—that the opinions and actions of other men control and direct him. Lastly, Crane dramatizes Fleming's realization that although he can project his emotions into natural phenomena and therefore derive comfort from a sense of nature's identification with his desires and needs, nature and man are really two, not one, and nature offers no reliable or useful guide to experience or to action. But, despite Crane's perception of these limitations and inadequacies, he does not paint a totally bleak picture of man in *The Red Badge*. True, Fleming's own sanguine view of himself at the close of the novel—that he is a man—cannot be taken at face value. Fleming's self-evaluations contrast ironically with his motives and actions throughout the novel, and his final estimation of himself represents primarily man's ability to be proud of his public deeds while rationalizing his private failings.

But something has happened to Fleming which Crane values and applauds. Early in the novel Fleming feels at odds with his comrades. He is separated from them by doubts about his behavior under fire and by fear of their knowledge of his doubts. These doubts and fears isolate him from his fellows, and his isolation is intensified by his growing awareness that the repressive power of the "moving box" of his regiment binds him to a group from which he now wishes to escape. Once in battle, however, Fleming becomes "not a man but a member" as he is "welded into a common personality which was dominated by a single desire." [271] The "subtle battle brotherhood" [272] replaces his earlier isolation, and in one sense the rest of the novel is devoted to Fleming's loss and recovery of his feeling of oneness with his fellows. After his initial success in battle, Henry loses this quality as he deserts his comrades and then wanders away from his regiment in actuality and in spirit. His extreme stage of isolation from the regiment and from mankind occurs when he abandons the tattered soldier. After gaining a "red badge" which symbolically reunites him with those soldiers who remained and fought, he returns to his regiment and participates successfully in the last stages of the battle. Here, as everywhere in Crane, there is a deflating irony, for Henry's "red badge" is not a true battle wound. But despite the tainted origin of this symbol of fraternity, its effect on Henry and his fellows is real and significant. He is accepted gladly when he returns, and in his renewed confidence and pride he finds strength and a kind of joy. Crane believed that this feeling of trust and mutual confidence among men is essential, and it is one of the few values he confirms again and again in his fiction. It is this quality which knits together the four men in the open boat and lends them moral strength. And it is the absence of this quality and its replacement by fear and distrust which characterizes the world of "The Blue Hotel" and causes the tragic denouement in that story.

Crane thus points out that courage has primarily a social reality, that it is a quality which exists not absolutely but by virtue of other men's opinions, and that the social unity born of a courageous fellowship may therefore be based on self-deception or on deception of others. He also demonstrates that this bond of fellowship may be destructive and oppressive when it restricts or determines individual choice, as in the "moving box" of the regiment. Fleming, after all, at first stands fast because he is afraid of what his comrades will do or think, and then runs because he feels that the rest of the regiment is deserting as well. But Crane also maintains that in social cohesion man gains both what little power of self-preservation he possesses and a gratifying and necessary sense of acceptance and acknowledgement difficult to attain otherwise. Crane therefore establishes a vital organic relationship between his deflation of the traditional idea of courage and his assertion of the need for and the benefits of social unity. He attacks the conventional heroic ideal by showing that a man's actions in battle are usually determined by his imitation of the actions of others—by the group as a whole. But this presentation of the reality and power of the group also suggests the advantages possible in group unity and group action.

There is, then, a moral ambiguity in Crane's conception of man's relationship with his fellows, an ambiguity which permeates his entire vision of man. Henry Fleming falsely acquires a symbol of group identity, yet this symbol aids him in recovering his group identity and in benefiting the group. Man's involvement with others forces him into psychic compulsion (Henry's running away), yet this involvement is the source of his sense of psychic oneness. Henry is still for the most part self-deceived at the close of the novel, but if he is not the "man" he thinks he has become, he has at least shed some of the innocence of the child. Crane's allegory of life as a battle is thus appropriate for another reason besides its relevance to the violence of discovery. Few battles are clearly or cleanly won or lost, and few soldiers are clearly God's chosen. But men struggle, and in their struggle they learn something about their limitations and capacities and something about the nature of their relations with their fellow men, and this knowledge is rewarding even though they never discover the full significance or direction of the campaign in which they are engaged.

v

The primary goal of the late nineteenth-century American naturalists was not to demonstrate the overwhelming and oppressive reality of the material forces present in our lives. Their attempt, rather, was to represent the intermingling in life of controlling force and individual worth. If they were not always clear in distinguishing between these two qualities in experience, it was partly because they were novelists responding to life's complexities and were not philosophers categorizing experience, and partly because they were sufficiently of our own time to doubt the validity of moral or any other absolutes. The naturalists do not dehumanize man. They rather suggest new or modified areas of value in man while engaged in destroying such old and to them unreal sources of human self-importance as romantic love or moral responsibility or heroism. They are some distance from traditional Christian humanism, but they have not yet reached the despairing emptiness of Joseph Wood Krutch's *The Modern Temper*. One should not deny the bleak view of man inherent in McTeague's or Hurstwood's decline or in Fleming's self-deceptions, but neither should one forget that to the naturalists man's weaknesses and limited knowledge and thwarted desires were still sources of compassion and worth, as well as aspects of the human condition to be more forthrightly acknowledged than writers had done in the past.

Nor is naturalism simply a piling on of unselective blocks of documentation. A successful naturalistic novel is like any successful work of art in that it embodies a cogent relationship between its form (its particular combination of the commonplace and sensational) and its theme (its particular tension between the individually significant and the deterministic).

There is a major difference, within general similarities, between Norris's discovery of the sensational in the commonplace and Crane's dramatization of the triviality of the sensational. This variation derives principally from the differing thematic tension in the two novels. Norris wishes to demonstrate the tragic destruction of McTeague's commonplace world by the violence inherent in all life, whereas Crane wishes to dramatize Fleming's violent initiation into the commonplace nature of the heroic. Norris and Crane occupy positions in American naturalism analogous to that of Wordsworth and Byron in English romanticism. Like the poetry of the two earlier figures, their fiction expresses strikingly individual and contrasting visions of experience, yet does so within a body of shared intellectual and literary assumptions belonging to their common historical and literary moment. The naturalistic novel is thus no different from any other major literary genre in its complex intermingling of form and theme, in its reflection of an author's individual temperament and experience within large generic similarities, and—at its best—in its thematic depth and importance. We have done a disservice to the late nineteenth-century American naturalists by our earlier simplistic conception of their art.

3 FRANK NORRIS'S
DEFINITION OF NATURALISM

FRANK NORRIS'S DEFINITION of naturalism is important because an understanding of his use of the term may help to explain both his own practice of fiction and the more general American reaction to Zolaesque literary principles. My reason for reintroducing the much-debated question of Norris's definition is that I believe new light can be shed on the subject by the examination of not only his well-known "A Plea for Romantic Fiction," but also his less-known "Zola as a Romantic Writer" and his relatively unknown "Weekly Letter" in the *Chicago American* of August 3, 1901.[1]

Norris placed realism, romanticism, and naturalism in a dialectic, in which realism and romanticism were opposing forces, and naturalism was transcending synthesis. Realism, to Norris, was the literature of the normal and representative, "the smaller details of every-day life, things that are likely to happen between lunch and supper . . . ."[2] Moreover, realism does not probe the inner reaches of life; it "notes only the surface of things."[3] Howells is Norris's archetype of the realistic writer. Romanticism differs from realism both in its concern for "variations from the type of normal life,"[4] and in its desire to penetrate beneath the surface of experience and derive large generalizations on the nature of life. Romanticism explores "the unplumbed depths of the human heart, and the mystery of sex, and the problems of life, and the black, unsearched penetralia of the soul of man." [5] To Norris "the greatest of all modern romanticists" is Hugo.[6]

Now what of naturalism? Although Norris at times called Zola a romanticist, it is clear that he intended in that designation to emphasize Zola's lack of affinity to Howellsian realism rather than to eliminate naturalism as a distinctive descriptive term.[7] Naturalism, as conceived by Norris, resolved the conflict between realism and romanticism by selecting the best from these two modes and by adding one constituent ignored by both. In his "Weekly Letter" to the *Chicago American* of August 3, 1901, he partially described this synthesis. He began with a distinction between Accuracy and Truth. Accuracy is fidelity to particular detail; Truth is fidelity to the generalization applicable to a large body of experience. Since a novel may therefore be accurate in its depiction of a segment of life and yet be untrue, Norris inquired what is the source of truth in fiction, if a literal transcription of life itself is inadequate. He began to find his way out of this dilemma when he asked;

> Is it permissible to say that Accuracy is realism and Truth romanticism? I am not so sure, but I feel that we come close to a solution here. The divisions seem natural and intended. It is not difficult to be accurate, but it is monstrously difficult to be True; at best the romanticists can only aim at it, while on the other hand, mere accuracy as an easily obtainable result is for that reason less worthy.[8]

Norris then asked;

> Does Truth after all "lie in the middle?" And what school, then, is midway between the Realists and Romanticists, taking the best from each? Is it not the school of Naturalism, which strives hard for accuracy

and truth? The nigger is out of the fence at last, but must it not be admitted that the author of *La Débâcle* (not the author of *La Terre* and *Fécondité*) [9] is up to the present stage of literary development the most adequate, the most satisfactory, the most just of them all? [10]

Naturalism, in short, abstracts the best from realism and romanticism—detailed accuracy and philosophical depth. In addition, naturalism differs from both modes in one important characteristic of its subject matter. As Norris explained in his *Wave* essay on "Zola as a Romantic Writer":

> That Zola's work is not purely romantic as was Hugo's, lies chiefly in the choice of Milieu. These great, terrible dramas no longer happen among the personnel of a feudal and Renaissance nobility, those who are in the fore-front of the marching world, but among the lower—almost the lowest—classes; those who have been thrust or wrenched from the ranks, who are falling by the roadway. This is not romanticism—this drama of the people, working itself out in blood and ordure. It is not realism. It is a school by itself, unique, somber, powerful beyond words. It is naturalism.[11]

What is particularly absorbing in this definition is that it is limited entirely to subject matter and method. It does not mention materialistic determinism or any other philosophical idea, and thus differs from the philosophical orientation both of Zola's discussions of naturalism and of those by modern critics of the movement.[12] Norris conceived of naturalism as a fictional mode which illustrated some fundamental truth of life within a detailed presentation of the sensational and low. Unlike Zola, however, he did not specify the exact nature of the truth to be depicted, and it is clear that he believed Hugo's "truth" as naturalistic as Zola's. With Norris's definition in mind, then, we can perhaps understand his remark to Isaac Marcosson that *The Octopus* was going to be a return to the "style" of *McTeague*—"straight naturalism." [13] Although the first novel is consciously deterministic in its treatment of human action and the second dramatizes a complex intermingling of free will and determinism, this contradiction is nonexistent within the philosophical vacuum of Norris's definition.

Norris's definition, however, is not only significant for his own fictional practice. It also clarifies some fundamental characteristics of the naturalistic movement in America. It suggests that for many Americans influenced by European naturalistic currents, the naturalistic mode involved primarily the contemporary, low, and sensational, which was elaborately documented within a large thematic framework. The writer might give his work a philosophical center—indeed, the naturalistic mode encouraged such a practice. But the core ideas or values present in particular works tended to be strikingly diverse from author to author, as each writer approached his material from an individual direction rather than from the direction of an ideological school. American naturalism, in other words, has been largely a movement characterized by similarities in material and method, not by philosophical coherence. And perhaps this very absence of a philosophical center to the movement has been one of the primary reasons for its continuing strength in this country, unlike its decline in Europe. For writers as different as Dreiser and Crane, or Farrell and Faulkner, have responded to the exciting possibilities of a combination of romantic grandioseness, detailed verisimilitude, and didactic sensationalism, and yet, like Norris, have been able to shape these possibilities into works expressing most of all their own distinctive temperaments.

4   THE EVOLUTIONARY FOUNDATION OF W. D. HOWELLS'S *CRITICISM AND FICTION*

WILLIAM DEAN HOWELLS'S *Criticism and Fiction* has never fared well as literary criticism, though its historical importance has seldom been questioned. In its own time it was a major contribution to the realism-romanticism controversy of the eighties and nineties. As in much literary dispute, examination of the work was usually neglected for criticism based upon a defense of vested literary interests or an a priori antagonism to the new and seemingly radical.[1] Today, the depreciation of *Criticism and Fiction* continues, though of course along different lines. Critics have found the source of its defects in the facts of its composition and publication. The volume was made up of brief, loosely connected critical essays which had originally appeared in other contexts in Howells's "Editor's Study" department in *Harper's Monthly*. Everett Carter, for example, considers it a "hastily contrived product of the scissors and the pastepot" lacking clarity and unity.[2] He also contends that Howells's literary principles changed sufficiently from January, 1886 (the date of the first "Editor's Study") to May, 1891 (when *Criticism and Fiction* was published) to invalidate not only the famous "smiling aspects of life" passage but the entire work as well. He points out that during 1886–87 Howells underwent the "agony" of the Haymarket affair and its resultant change in his social and literary views. *Criticism and Fiction*, which contains material written both before and after this crisis, is therefore not an adequate expression of Howells's mature critical realism. He concludes that one has "to look elsewhere for the best expression of his critical opinions." [3]

There is no doubt that *Criticism and Fiction* adversely reflects its original periodical publication. There are obvious transitional gaps and contrivances; the work lacks outward direction and focus; and there is much repetition. But this is not to say that the collection is deficient in a coherent, pervasive, and unified system of ideas which serves as an intellectual base for Howells's critical attitudes. It is a belief in the evolution of literature which underlies the seemingly disparate critical comments of *Criticism and Fiction*. I will first examine the general nature of the use of evolutionary ideas in literary criticism during the 1880's and Howells's own awareness and acceptance of this use.[4] I will then indicate the foundation of evolutionary ideas in *Criticism and Fiction*. It should be clear, however, that my analysis of *Criticism and Fiction* is not a defense of its two paramount weaknesses—an undisciplined structure and an overreliance, for polemic purposes, upon the contemporary belief that evolutionary theories could be applied to an interpretation of literature. Rather, my purpose is to point out the depth of Howells's dependence upon this belief and to indicate that his attitudes toward criticism and fiction are coherent in their common reference to a conception of the evolution of literature.

ii

Perhaps one of the clearest and also most doctrinaire examples of evolutionary literary criticism is an unpublished work by Hamlin Garland, written during 1886–87, entitled "The Evolution of American Thought."[5] At one point in this history of American literature, Garland wrote: "Nothing is stable, nothing absolute, all changes, all is relative. Poetry, painting, the drama, these too are always being modified or left behind by the changes in society from which they spring."[6] This statement contains two of the main tenets of evolutionary criticism—that literature is a product of the society in which it is found; and that literature, like society, is therefore continually in flux. To this basic environment relativism can be added the idea that change in both society and literature is slowly but inevitably progressive. "The golden age is here and now," Garland summed up, "and the future is a radiant promise of ineffable glory."[7] The primary sources of these ideas, for Garland and for other evolutionary critics of the period, are not far to seek. From Taine came the principle that literature is conditioned by the forces of race, environment, and epoch. From evolutionary science, which itself reinforced an environmental determinism, came the idea that life is continually in flux. And from such popularizers of evolution as Herbert Spencer and John Fiske came the belief that the principle of change was applicable to social, intellectual, and moral—as well as material—life and was characterized by the ultimate achievement of "the greatest perfection and the most complete happiness."[8]

Garland had been influenced directly by Taine and Spencer and also, to a lesser extent, by the criticism of Hutcheson Macaulay Posnett and Thomas Sergeant Perry, two evolutionary critics whose work was also known by Howells. In the Preface to his *Comparative Literature* (1886), Posnett stated that his purpose was "to explain literary development by scientific principles."[9] The use of these principles involved grouping the study of literature

round certain central facts of comparatively permanent
influence. Such facts are the climate, soil, animal and
plant life of different countries; such also is the principle
of evolution from communal to individual life. . . .
The former may be called the statical influences to
which literature has been everywhere exposed; the latter may be called the dynamical principle of literature's
progress and decay.[10]

These two "facts"—obviously derived from Taine and
Spencer—led Posnett to his central critical belief, that
there are no absolutes in literary form or content. For,
he argued, given the fact that literature depends on
physical and social conditions and that these conditions vary in time and place, how can one maintain
that there are absolute standards? Social life had
evolved progressively from the homogeneity of the
clan to the heterogeneity of a modern democracy. And
since literature, if it is to be vital, must reflect this
progress, it is retrogressive to ask the modern writer to
conform to standards which were derived by older
civilizations. In the body of his work Posnett examined
the progress of world literature from barbaric times to
his own day and concluded with a celebration of
Whitman's "democratic individualism."

Both Garland and Posnett were disciples of Herbert
Spencer and attempted to apply Spencerian evolutionary formulas to an interpretation of the "dynamic" in
literature. But T. S. Perry, although he too was
influenced by Spencer, revealed that it was not necessary to use a particular evolutionary system, that an
awareness of literature's change and growth could
constitute an evolutionary method. His *English Literature in the Eighteenth Century* (1883), for example,
was an attempt to illustrate "the more evident laws
that govern literature." [11] He was at particular pains, in
his Preface, to refute Mrs. Oliphant's *Literary History*

*of England in the End of the Eighteenth and Begin-
ning of the Nineteenth Century* (1882). Mrs. Oliphant had accepted the idea of progress in most phases
of life but had denied its applicability to literature and
art because there had been no advance upon Shakespeare or Fra Angelico. Perry, like most evolutionary
critics, conceded that the source and nature of genius
were inexplicable. But he argued that genius is nevertheless conditioned by life and that the general drift
of life was progressive. The writer

> can see only what exists or may exist, and is limited by
> experience whether this be treated literally or be
> modified by the imagination. No writer can escape this
> limitation any more than he can imagine a sixth sense. If
> these statements are accurate, and a general, although
> not uniform, progress is acknowledged to exist in society,
> literature may also be said to be under the sway of law,
> or, rather, to move in accordance with law.[12]

Like Garland and Posnett, Perry accepted the premises
and conclusion of the evolutionary critical syllogism:
that literature is conditioned by society; that society
progresses; and therefore that literature progresses in
the "general widening of human interest and sympathies" which it mirrors, though a genius may be lacking
to crystallize this progress into great expression.[13]

But Perry's conception of the "laws that govern
literature" contained in addition an idea which was to
play an important role in Howells's treatment of literary progress. Perry believed that the progress of society
was reflected in literature. But he also accepted John
Addington Symonds's belief that literary genres occupied the position of species within the broad pattern of
progress and that each genre passed through a life cycle
of birth, maturity, and decay.[14] The advantage of this
dual conception was that it allowed Perry to postulate
the perpetual progress of society and literature, yet also

supplied him with an explanation (one of several) for fluctuation in the history of literature. Shakespeare was a genius extant at the apex of his genre's cycle. There might have been comparable geniuses at earlier or later periods in the history of Elizabethan drama, but they were unfortunately limited by the immaturity or decay of the genre. As Perry explained in discussing the Greek drama, Sophocles reached a higher level of achievement than Aeschylus, but the difference between them was "not so much a personal one as it was the necessary result of their relative positions in the history of the Greek drama." [15]

This duality in the conception of the evolution of literature also had the advantage of permitting Perry to establish permanent critical values despite the relativism caused by literature's dependence upon a society continually in flux. Indeed, the relationship between literature and society was the source of these values, for a close relationship was necessary if literature was to represent the progress of society. The progress in any literary genre was therefore not only a growth in technique and form, but also a more truthful representation of the life of its time. Decay occurred when this latter function was neglected or when another genre more able to perform the task arose.

Several recent studies have documented Howells's knowledge of science and his acceptance of evolutionary ideas, and there is no need for more than a summary here.[16] During his years as an editor and then editor-in-chief of the *Atlantic Monthly* (1866–81), Howells read, reviewed, or editorially supervised many works and articles on Taine and evolution. During these years he also became closely acquainted with John Fiske and Perry, both of whom were Cambridge neighbors and contributors to the *Atlantic*.[17] By the time he began writing the "Editor's Study," Howells fully supported an evolutionary interpretation of literature. In a review of Posnett's *Comparative Literature* in the July, 1886, "Editor's Study," he applauded both Posnett and Perry for their "application of scientific theories to literature" and for their "conscious perception of principles which others have been feeling more or less blindly, and which are really animating and shaping the whole future of criticism." Both critics, he pointed out, hold that "literature is from life, and that it is under the law as every part of life is, and is not a series of preposterous miracles." [18] And in reviews later that year and in 1891 he continued to praise Perry's "scientific methods" which indicate "a new voice, a new temper" in literary criticism.[19]

iii

Criticism and Fiction has little external pattern, but what organization it has suggests its controlling current of ideas. The work consists of an unnumbered introduction and twenty-eight numbered essays. The twenty-eight essays can be divided into two parts: the first thirteen deal primarily with criticism, the last fifteen with fiction. The introductory unnumbered essay is taken up almost entirely with a passage from J. A. Symonds's *Renaissance in Italy*, which Howells quoted as relevant to the problem of establishing enduring critical principles in literature as well as in art. Symonds hopefully anticipated that criticism in the future would avoid " 'sentimental or academical seekings after the ideal' " and " 'momentary theories founded upon idiosyncratic or temporary partialities.' " Once this has been accomplished, the role of the critic will be that of " 'a healthy person who has made himself acquainted with the laws of evolution in art and in society, and is able to test the excellence of work in any stage from immaturity to decadence by discerning what there is of truth, sincerity, and natural vigor in it.' " [20] In short, the equipment of the critic will be a rejection of the older critical standards of the ideal and the personal, an acceptance of the principle of evolution in society and literature, and a realization that truth, sincerity, and vigor are the most estimable qualities of literature. Howells's strategic placing of this excerpt encourages the belief that these were to be the methods of his own examination of modern criticism and fiction.

A fundamental postulate of an evolutionary critical system is that literature is a product of the physical, social, and intellectual environment in which it is found and can best be understood and interpreted in terms of its environment. Howells accepted this belief, giving it a nationalistic or racial emphasis, as Taine had done. He explained that the "dispassionate, scientific student" of literature realizes that "it is a plant which springs from the nature of a people, and draws its forces from their life, that its root is in their character, and that it takes form from their will and taste." [55]

Howells also accepted the other major postulates of an evolutionary system—that both society and literature are characterized by change for the better. Society was not only advancing materially, but was achieving a greater humanitarianism and a submersion of the primitive and bestial. Literature also was both mutable and progressive. Fiction, for example, was progressing in two ways, one internally, the other a reflection of progress in society. Internally, in form and technique, it had gradually evolved from crudity and obviousness to subtlety, complexity, and sureness of touch. In subject matter it had increasingly devoted itself to a truthful and sincere account of the affairs of mankind. Society's growing humanitarianism was mirrored in the novel's concern for the truth in human relations in every sphere of life.

Realism was the fictional method which embodied

both the technical and the humanitarian progress of fiction. Howells confessed that he liked "better to go forward than to go backward, and it is saying very little to say that I value more such a novel as Mr. James's *Tragic Muse* than all the romantic attempts since Hawthorne." [118] He believed that the movement from classicism to romanticism to realism was a kind of positivistic progress toward a literature which would attempt to describe life truthfully:

> Romanticism then sought [in its struggle against classicism], as realism seeks now, to widen the bounds of sympathy, to level every barrier against aesthetic freedom, to escape from the paralysis of tradition. It exhausted itself in this impulse; and it remained for realism to assert that fidelity to experience and probability of motive are essential conditions of a great imaginative literature. It is not a new theory, but it has never before universally characterized literary endeavor. [15]

Howells's conception of the novel as a developing genre is illustrated by his evaluation of the great novelists of the preceding age. Balzac, Scott, and Dickens were literary geniuses who were nevertheless restricted by the primitive state of the novel during their age. The novel was a slowly progressing species with a particular norm of achievement at a particular moment in time; even the great man could not vary too much from the norm. The barbarian who discovered fire was a genius and was greater than those around him, but he was still a barbarian. "In the beginning of any art even the most gifted worker must be crude in his methods . . . ." [21] Writers in the "stone age" [119] of fiction, however, such as Scott and Balzac, were not to be condemned for their flaws in technique and content. Balzac "stood at the beginning of the great things that have followed since in fiction . . . [but] one perceives that Balzac lived too soon to profit by Balzac." [18–19] His technique was "not so bad in

him as it would be in a novelist of our day. It is simply
primitive and inevitable, and he is not to be judged by
it." [20] Even Goethe in his fiction could not rise
above the low development of the novel during his age:
"What is useful in any review of Goethe's methods is
the recognition of the fact . . . that the greatest master cannot produce a masterpiece in a new kind. The
novel was too recently invented in Goethe's day not to
be, even in his hands, full of the faults of apprentice
work." [24]

iv

There remains the primary question of
Howells's application of his conception of the evolution of fiction to the contemporary roles of criticism
and fiction. Howells assigned criticism a scientific role;
its function was not to direct or control the progress of
fiction, but rather to describe and analyze fiction on
the basis of a realization of the law of progress as it
operated in society and literature. Fiction, on the other
hand, was creatively to embody a truthful description
of contemporary life.

Howells's limitation of the function of criticism
denied to it, above all, the right of judgment. The
critic had not realized that "it is really his business to
classify and analyze the fruits of the human mind very
much as the naturalist classifies the objects of his
study, rather than to praise or blame them . . . ."
[30] Most contemporary criticism was marred by judgment based upon personal taste or party and literary
prejudice. Too much criticism, moreover, was merely a
display of wit and brilliance, in the English fashion.

Howells restricted the role of criticism because it
had retarded, by judgments based upon false standards, the natural progress of fiction. In the modern
period it was beginning to be seen "that no author is an

authority except in those moments when he held his ear close to Nature's lips and caught her very accent." [14] But despite this realization, "criticism does not inquire whether a work is true to life, but tacitly or explicitly compares it with models and tests it by them." [47] Too many readers, misled by criticism and unaware that literature progressed, desired the "ideal grasshopper, the heroic grasshopper, the impassioned grasshopper" [12] which they recalled from the authors of their youth. They judged modern fiction therefore "by a standard taken from these authors, and never dreamed of judging it by nature." [12–13]

Modern criticism was to a large measure responsible for this "petrifaction of taste" which represented a more primitive level of both art and life. Criticism wished literary art to "travel in a vicious circle" rather than a straight line, and to "arrive only at the point of departure." [47] In other words, criticism as a genre was backward; it had not developed sufficiently to realize its place and function. It was distinctly atavistic, for example, in its continuance of anonymous criticism, a "savage condition" which "still persists" despite the advance of manners and courtesy in society. [50] But most of all, criticism had not realized that principles and laws function in literature as well as in every phase of life.

Fortunately, the main tendency in world fiction had been progressive, despite the hindrance of much criticism. If criticism still failed to recognize the intrinsic relationship between life and literature, this was not true of most modern fiction. Fiction of the past, however, had been "largely injurious . . . through its falsehood, its folly, its wantonness, and its aimlessness." [93–94] It was therefore a sign of progress that the modern novel was required to answer the question, "Is it true?—true to the motives, the impulses, the principles that shape the life of actual men and women?" [99] Truth was now the "highest mission" of fiction, and though modern fiction was not always equal to the task, "fiction is now a finer art than it has ever been hitherto, and more nearly meets the requirements of the infallible standard." [185–86] This did not mean that fiction was the ultimate form, that it alone could meet the standards of truth and sincerity. On the contrary, it was conceivable that

> when the great mass of readers, now sunk in the foolish joys of mere fable, shall be lifted to an interest in the meaning of things through the faithful portrayal of life in fiction, then fiction the most faithful may be superseded by a still more faithful form of contemporaneous history. [186–87]

In short, progress was along the line of an increasingly truthful portrayal of life, not only within a genre, but from genre to genre as well.

But if the novel was progressing, why was there so much that was false and romantic in modern fiction? And why, particularly, had English fiction decayed since Jane Austen, who had been "the first and the last" English novelist to treat material with complete truthfulness and was "alone worthy to be matched with the great Scandinavian and Slavic and Latin artists"? [73] As far as the English novel was concerned, this arresting of progress was "not a question of intellect, or not wholly that. The English have mind enough; but they have not taste enough; or, rather, their taste has been perverted by their false criticism, which is based upon personal preference, and not upon principle . . . ." [73–74] Of course, the "taint" of romanticism had adversely affected the English novel after Austen and was partially responsible for its decline—"but it really seems as if it were their criticism that was to blame for the rest: not, indeed, for the performance of this writer or that, . . . but for the esteem in which this writer or that is held through the perpetuation of false ideals." [75] The English novel had suffered from the failure of English criticism to realize the principles which govern criticism and fiction and was an outstanding example of the ability of false criticism to hinder the progress of fiction.

With the exception of England, world fiction was advancing in meeting the tests of truth and sincerity. But despite this general advance, Howells noted that certain older, "untruthful" forms of fiction continued to remain popular. He explained that these older types were primitive forms of entertainment which appealed to those who in "every civilized community live in a state of more or less evident savagery." [109] Moreover, even "the most refined, the most enlightened person has his moods, his moments of barbarism. . . . At these times the lettered and the unlettered are alike primitive . . . ." [109] The romanticist still appealed because "the world often likes to forget itself, and he brings on his heroes, his goblins, his feats . . . and the poor, foolish, childish old world renews the excitements of its nonage." [107] Though Howells himself acknowledged some pleasure in poetical and historical romances, he admonished that the reader was not to confuse these survivals with the true function of modern fiction; otherwise "we shall be in danger of becoming permanently part of the 'unthinking multitude,' and of remaining puerile, primitive, savage." [111]

One of Howells's principal concerns in *Criticism and Fiction* was to examine the state of contemporary American fiction. He found that on the whole it was playing its role in the progress of world fiction and was representing American life with increasing truthfulness, sincerity, and vigor. American novels, unlike English, had "a disposition to regard our life without the literary glasses so long thought desirable, and to see character, not as it is in other fiction, but as it abounds outside of all fiction." [124]

American fiction, since it viewed American life truthfully, reflected the actual conditions of American life. Howells pointed out that most attacks on American fiction were invalid because the supposed weaknesses were the product of American conditions. American fiction, for example, lacked the tragic depth of a Dostoevsky because our life consisted primarily of "well-to-do actualities." [129] The idea of the average, the norm, was important here as elsewhere in Howells's conception of the role of American fiction. The writer concerned himself, in his attempt to arrive at the closest possible approximation of the truth, with the most probable, the most characteristic, rather than the anomaly, which might be true to one but not to the average.

Howells's belief that literature more closely approaches truth as it devotes itself to the norm of behavior appears most clearly in his analysis of the treatment of sex in American fiction. He acknowledged that the American novel dealt less openly with sex than either eighteenth-century English or contemporary French fiction. But he considered this absence an advance on two levels. On the one hand, the American novel was again reflecting the progress of society, for the "manners of the novel have been improving with those of its readers." [154] But also, American fiction, by subordinating sex, more accurately represented the true position of sex in life. Contemporary novelists had not denied the role of sex and passion, but had rather "relegated them in their pictures of life to the space and place they occupy in life itself, as we know it in England and America. They have kept a correct proportion . . . ." [156]

Another charge against American fiction which Howells refuted was that it was too narrow. Here again he pointed out that the supposed defect was actually a virtue, since it indicated a truthful representation of a condition of American life. American novels were still thorough, but their

> breadth is vertical instead of lateral, that is all; and this depth is more desirable than horizontal expansion in a civilization like ours, where the differences are not of classes, but of types, and not of types either so much as of characters. A new method was necessary in dealing with the new conditions . . . . [142]

No writer could hope to capture all of American life—"our social and political decentralization forbids this" [144]—and specialization had become necessary.

Lastly, Howells traced the relationship between a democracy and the literature which reflected it. American life had been derided for lacking distinction. But Howells saw such a deficiency as a source of inspiration, not discouragement, for the American writer. American life affirmed "the essential equality of men in their rights and duties." [139] This democratic condition invited the artist "to the study and the appreciation of the common, and to the portrayal in every art of those finer and higher aspects which unite rather than sever humanity, if he would thrive in our new order of things." [139] In his truthful study of the common, the American writer was not to gloss over the inadequacies of American life, its poor and suffering. A truthful fiction describing these weaknesses aided in their amelioration, since it forced men to respond to the spirit of brotherhood implicit in a democracy: "Men are more like than unlike one another; let us make them know one another better, that they may be all humbled and strengthened with a sense of their fraternity." [188] A democratic fiction which would reflect both the fraternity and the lapses from fraternity in American life would be a high-water mark in the progress of fiction.

v

Criticism and Fiction is no more than a fraction of Howells's total critical writings, and it is perhaps unrepresentative in its polemicism and overstatement, which were products of the atmosphere of controversy in which the original essays were written. Yet the work, despite the additional facts that it is hastily contrived and that it spans a period of vital change in Howells's social views, is nevertheless an adequate representation of his critical position. Howells believed throughout his later career as well as in 1886 that American fiction progressed as it came closer to a truthful portrayal of American life, and that it was the role of criticism to aid, rather than hinder, this progress. It was Howells's perception of American life—that the smiling aspects were not as characteristic as he had supposed—which changed, not his conception of the functions of criticism and fiction.

But *Criticism and Fiction* also illustrates some of the dangers of the application of a doctrinaire theory—"scientific" or otherwise—to literary criticism. Howells found in evolution a means of defending Howellsian realism and attacking his *bêtes noires* of English criticism and romantic fiction. Perhaps such an adaptation is the fate of most sociological or biological theories which are applied to the study of literature in a controversial context. But evolution—which encouraged the critic to select contemporary modes and forms and then to interpret literature as a "progress" toward these goals—was apparently particularly susceptible to this temptation.

THOMAS SERGEANT PERRY (1845–1928) occupies a minor though secure niche in late nineteenth-century
American literary history. His lifelong friendships with
Henry James and William Dean Howells are often
recalled, as are his extensive and sympathetic reviews
of foreign literature during the 1870's. At a time when
Continental realism was still largely unknown and suspect, he championed many of the leading French and
Russian realists in the *Atlantic Monthly,* the *Nation,*
and the *North American Review.* In 1881 Perry's
position as a Harvard instructor was not renewed, and
in that same year Howells's resignation as editor of the
Atlantic deprived Perry of his connection with that
journal. Perry's release from both teaching and review-
ing prompted him to undertake more extensive and, he
hoped, more profitable critical works. The first of
these, *English Literature in the Eighteenth Century,*
was presented as a course of lectures during 1881–82
and was published in 1883. During the next five years
Perry wrote *From Opitz to Lessing: A Study of
Pseudo-Classicism in Literature* (1884), *The Evolution of the Snob* (1886), "The Progress of Literature"
(1886),[1] and *A History of Greek Literature* (1890).[2]
These works, however, succeeded neither financially
nor critically. In 1887 Perry went abroad for several

years, and for the rest of his long life he devoted himself primarily to travel and reading.

During the late 1860's and early 1870's, while Perry was a youthful tutor of French and German at Harvard, he came under the influence of evolutionary ideas. He became friends with his Cambridge neighbor John Fiske, and he joined The Club, the members of which were principally young teachers and writers of liberal and modern views. Perry's mind was essentially rationalistic and realistic. His dislike and distrust of the vague and abstract, of all philosophical theorizing, were notorious among his friends.[3] Moreover, he believed that all important ideas are simple—that the great truth is the one which clarifies and simplifies that which was complex and muddy.[4] Given this cast of mind and the age in which he lived, it is not surprising that Perry found in evolution a principle which would serve to clarify and to simplify the history of literature and which would free its study from what he believed were metaphysical and romantic vagaries. Some of the more obvious indications of his adoption of evolution as such a principle are his dedication of his first critical work to Fiske and his frequent call for the application of evolutionary ideas to the interpretation of literary history.[5] The less obvious indications are the concern of this essay, whose purpose it is to present a synthesized (rather than book by book) description of the conception of the evolution of literature which appears in Perry's work of the 1880's.[6] This description will cast light on the theoretical basis of Perry's defense of realism, a defense which was of some importance in the American literary scene of the 1870's and 1880's. For not only were Perry's reviews warmly responsive to the possibilities of realism, but he himself exerted a personal as well as a literary influence on such contemporary Boston figures as Howells and Hamlin Garland,

and on such a former-pupil-turned-critic as George Pellew. Perry's critical work of the 1880's is of interest, then, for two reasons. On the one hand, it is a noteworthy American example of the international phenomenon of the influence of evolutionary ideas on late nineteenth-century literary criticism. On the other, it is a clear example of the use of evolutionary ideas to support realism, an example which offers an insight into the major, though often less obvious, strand of evolutionary ideas in two important contemporary critical defenses of realism—Howells's *Criticism and Fiction* (1891) and Garland's *Crumbling Idols* (1894).

ii

In late 1882 Perry noted of the use of evolutionary ideas in literary studies that "It's magnificent to have a principle abt. wh. things arrange themselves. . . . It seems as if we had an unfailing touchstone in our hands, and that we cld. not fail to find the truth."[7] As interpreted by Perry, the primary characteristic of this principle was growth. Noting that "there are people who shudder if they hear *Darwinism* mentioned, and who have prejudices against the word *evolution*," he proposed that we "call it *growth*, and no one will be pained . . . ."[8] There was nothing "terrible" in evolution, he assured a friend, "it is merely the hypothesis that everything is a matter of *growth*, as opposed to the notion of special creations."[9]

The "everything" in Perry's definition is of importance. In his biography of Fiske, Perry recalled that one of the effects of the impact of evolutionary ideas was that "The world unrolled itself in a new harmony as one vast whole."[10] Literature was not a unique phenomenon. It was part of a universal process, governed by the same laws which governed every other aspect of life. Perry's conception of these laws was largely Spencerian, though he was always undoctrinaire in his use of Spencerian ideas.[11] Like Herbert Spencer, Perry believed that the principal characteristic of evolutionary growth was the progress of all life from incoherent homogeneity to coherent heterogeneity. In social evolution this movement took concrete form in the increasing concern for individual rights, a concern reflected in the rise of political democracy and religious freedom. Perry revealed his acceptance of a Spencerian conception of evolutionary progress when he wrote of the history of the drama:

> The change from a drama that represented only kings and heroes of princely birth to one that concerned itself with human beings, was as inevitable a thing as is the change in government from despotism to democracy. There is a certain monotony in civilization which may be exemplified in a thousand ways. The large gas pipes, for instance, that are laid in every street, and have the smaller branches running into every house, which again feed the ramifying tubes that supply the single lights, may remind one of the advance from the general to the particular which characterizes every form of human thought.[12]

Since this advance was universal, the function of the modern critic was the "scientific examination of . . . historical growth." [13] The widespread acceptance of this function was being hindered, however, by the continuing adoration of artistic genius, an obstacle parallel to that offered by special creation in the rise of evolutionary science. Perry noted that although the idea that it is possible to evoke "something out of nothing by direct exercise of creative power . . . has vanished from science, it still survives in those departments of human activity which have not yet come fully under scientific treatment, and poets and painters enjoy in the popular estimation a privilege which has been denied to nature." [14] Perry therefore frequently attacked the belief that genius was outside the "laws that govern literature." [15] In his Preface to *English Literature in the Eighteenth Century*, for example, he refuted Mrs. Oliphant's apotheosis of genius in her *Literary History of England in the End of the Eighteenth and the Beginning of the Nineteenth Century* (1882). " 'Every singer is a new miracle.' " Perry quoted Mrs. Oliphant, " 'created if nothing else is created—no growth developed out of precedent poets, but something sprung from an impulse which is not reducible to law.' " [16] To this Perry replied that, though the cause of genius was unknown, every artist, regardless of ability,

> is bound by the necessity of building on the foundations that society is laying every day. Every apparently insignificant action of ours contributes its mite to the sum of circumstances which inspire the writer, whose vision may be dim or inaccurate, but who can see only what exists or may exist, and is limited by experience whether this be treated literally or be modified by the imagination. No writer can escape this limitation any more than he can imagine a sixth sense. If these statements are accurate, and a general, although not uniform, progress is acknowledged to exist in society, literature may also be said to be under the sway of law, or, rather, to move in accordance with law. [17]

Of course, Perry realized the inherent weakness in any idea of literary progress, and he was quick to point out that "We shall not expect every later writer to be greater than Shakespeare." [18] The quantity and quality of genius in any age were unstable and unpredictable. What was stable and predictable, however, was the progress of society, and in modern life, "although the vivid genius is absent, there is a general widening of human interest and sympathies, which will be more apparent when it is crystallized by some great writer than it is now." [19]

One of the primary tools of the scientific critic was the comparative method. Parallels in the literatures of various countries were evidence that each nation's literary production was the result of that nation's particular stage of social and intellectual evolution. "All literary history teaches us that in different countries similar conditions produce similar work," Perry stated.[20] Every singer was not "a new miracle" when there were similar performers across the channel or on the other side of the Rhine. Perry's *From Opitz to Lessing* was largely an exercise in the comparative method. The aim of the work, he noted in his Preface, was "to give some few of the many available proofs that the different nations of modern Europe have passed through very nearly the same experience in literature since the Renaissance." [21]

The scientific critic, armed with the principle of growth and with the comparative method, realized that law rather than chance governed the history of literature. He perceived, moreover, that the law of literary growth was not confined to the limitation of literature by social evolution. It also affirmed that the literary work was conditioned by the evolution of its genre.

Perry conceived of the genre as a species with a life cycle from birth to maturity to ultimate decay. He appears to have derived this conception from John Addington Symonds, who frequently used it in his voluminous writings and whose work Perry valued highly.[22] As stated and applied by Symonds and Perry, the primary characteristic of the idea was the subservience of the artist to the stage of growth or decay of the genre in which he was participating. The law was particularly applicable to art prior to the seventeenth century, when genres were still "true," when they had not yet been "hybridized" by cross influences from other genres and other societies. Perry therefore made his greatest use of the idea in his *A History of Greek Literature*, in which he analyzed the major Greek literary genres in terms of growth and decay.

The history of each Greek literary genre, Perry believed, could best be described as a horizontal parabola. The appearance of a Homer writing a perfect epic (the apex of the parabola) implied a long, though now lost, history of less successful preparation for this event. "Every successful work implies a host of failures," Perry declared, and "what has at first seemed to be the product of some one half-inspired person has, when closely studied, turned out to be only the full development of a crude past." [23] Growth within a genre was from the general and abstract to the particular and concrete (another application of Spencerian ideas), while decay was a movement from the reflection of actual life to imitation and artificiality. The individual writer's work was determined by this pattern. Sophocles reached a higher level of achievement than Aeschylus, but the difference between them "was not so much a personal one as it was the necessary result of their relative positions in the history of the Greek drama." [24]

In his discussion of the Greek drama, Perry epitomized his conception of what might be called a literature of law, not men. "If the position of the three great tragedians had been altered," he wrote, "so that Euripides had been the oldest, and Aeschylus had been the youngest, it is not to be supposed that the development of the drama would have been exactly opposite to the form that we are now studying." [25] For the differences in the work of these dramatists were less the product of individual variation than "the state of the dramatic art and of society that created and presented the conditions under which these men worked." [26]

Evolutionary criticism therefore posited a twofold determinism. The work of the artist was determined by the social conditions of his time and by the genre in which he worked. The former were progressive; the latter described a curve from birth to death. Together, they constituted "a principle abt. wh. things arrange themselves." [27]

iii

The modern student of literature was similar to the modern scientist. Both sought a truthful description of the phenomenon under study, a description which precluded judgment. Perry suggested that "it is a question whether praise and blame, admiration and contempt, have anything whatsoever to do with literary history. Our sole aim should be to know." [28] But in practice Perry did establish and apply evaluative criteria. Like Taine, who also attempted to introduce a scientific methodology into literary study, he made his descriptive principles serve double duty as sources of value judgment. [29]

At one point in his Preface to *English Literature in the Eighteenth Century* Perry noted that despite Mrs. Oliphant's claim that literature did not advance, her own novels were proof of literary progress. They occupied "a normal position in the development of fiction, with their exact drawing of life and avoidance of direct moral teaching." [30] Both of these goals were implicit in Perry's conception of the evolution of literature. If literature was inseparable from the whole of life, the more it approximated life the more it fulfilled its natural role. Any literary work which was not derived from the contemporary life of its nation was artificial, imitative, or affected. Such a work subverted literature's position as part of the whole and therefore literature's progress as the whole of life progressed. In short, literature was not only describable in terms of the unity of all life, but could also be judged on the basis of its varying degree of reflection of that unity.

Perry condemned literature which did not mirror the life of its time and place. Such literature he pejoratively characterized as "literary" and "artistic," whereas literature which represented its era exhibited such praiseworthy "lifelike" qualities as simplicity, directness, and naturalness. That literature should be anything but "literary," he remarked, "may seem at first sight the height of paradox, especially when for centuries the aim of all cultivation has been to produce something that should be true to abstract principles of art, and hence as remote from life as everything intentionally unreal must always be." [31] But "what is best in all literature is the most natural form of expression," he declared, "a form that grows from the soil." [32]

Nondidacticism was an important quality of a literature derived directly from life, Perry believed. Life teaches best through experience rather than by means of an artificially imposed morality. Similarly, "every story, exactly in proportion to its truth to life, carries with it some lesson." [33] Didacticism in a genre was either a sign of immaturity (as in Samuel Richardson) or of retrogression (as in George Eliot's early work).

The principle of universal growth therefore served as both a descriptive framework and a source of evaluative standards. When combined, the description and the evaluation constituted an interpretative history of literature. Perry actually surveyed the history of world literature in "The Progress of Literature." But his other works, though they deal principally with Greek

and eighteenth-century literature, also contain numerous passages on most of the literary periods from the
ancient to the modern. Perry's work of the 1880's
reveals a coherent conception of the pattern of literary
history.

Literature had not been uniformly progressive, Perry
believed, despite the social and material advance of
mankind which had continually increased the potential of literary achievement. This potential remained
largely unfulfilled, however, since its very existence was
inadequately realized. Writers and critics had infre-
quently acknowledged the intrinsic relationship between literature and life, and literature had therefore
seldom availed itself of the opportunity of enrolling
itself in the progress of mankind. The history of literature and art, Perry wrote, was "a long record of the
obstacles that thwart simplicity and directness." [34]
Instead of literature's steady progress, Perry traced a
fluctuation dependent on the proximity of each age's
literature to its life.

Throughout his *History of Greek Literature* Perry
emphasized that the greatness of Greek literature
stemmed from two interdependent causes—its reliance
on Greek life and its freedom from literary conventions. "Of no people is it truer than of the Greeks," he
stated, "that their literature is not an artificial product,
but the race speaking. The most important thing to
remember in studying their writings is that these are
the direct expression of a free people, leading its own
life, untrammeled by inherited rules or authoritative
convention." [35] With the Greeks "literature was, as it
should be, as broad as life itself; belief and doubt, joy
and sorrow, enthusiasm and contempt, all found natural expression without reference to a literary code." [36]
Greek literature began to decay when it neglected
"natural expression" for literary refinement and be-

came a "mechanical art." [37] This decay continued into Latin literature, which adopted imitation as a mode. During the middle ages the "general enfeeblement of active interests" was reflected in "the gradual evaporation of literature." [38]

The "clearing away of the middle ages" began in the Renaissance.[39] The initial effect of the rediscovery of classic literature was a beneficial stimulation of literary enthusiasm. But the ultimate effect was harmful, for "When this first fervor died out, and people turned to books for directions about writing rather than for a sympathetic glow, the rules were deemed of the utmost importance, pedants got into power, and pseudo-classicism held full sway over the literature and taste of modern Europe," [40] During the later English Renaissance, only the stage remained vital. "The great dramatists held their position by reason of their close relation with the people." [41] But literature on the whole "had broken loose from the people, and had to seek support from the court," where affectation and imitation became the rule.[42]

European literature rejected life for almost a century and a half following the Renaissance. "Formal correctness" based on Latin models resulted in a literary authoritarianism which Perry equated with political and religious authoritarianism, particularly in France, where "the idea of submission to authority" dominated all thought.[43] The romantic movement was initially a rejection of authority in the name of an emotionally grasped belief in personal liberty. Like the Renaissance, however, after an initial burst of freshness and naturalness, it too fell into the errors of conventionality and "literary artifice." [44]

Despite its decline, the romantic movement was important for introducing an "assertion of man's individuality" into the stream of ideas.[45] Although the romantic statement of man's individuality was often inflated and sentimental, it nevertheless laid the foundations for the antagonism to authority characteristic of modern life and literature. And from modern antiauthoritarianism there had emerged the climate of freedom necessary for a return to life as a source of literary inspiration and material.

Perhaps even more important than romantic individualism as a source of literary antiauthoritarianism was the rise of science. "Freedom is the very breath of science," Perry declared, "and the general free movement of boundless human curiosity cannot fail to affect literature." [46] The climate of freedom derived from science had already influenced literature in two important ways. Encouraged to disregard literary conventions and rules, the writer was again turning to life and was attempting to represent life with the accuracy and the fidelity to experience which an age of science demanded. And he found in life, and therefore reflected, a desire for freedom from political and social authoritarianism analogous to his own desire for literary freedom. "The movement in letters in the present day," Perry summed up, "is in the direction of scientific exactness and democracy, which are two indications of the freedom which civilization is acquiring." [47]

Realism was the contemporary mode which embodied this movement. "After all," Perry argued, "what can realism produce but the downfall of conventionality? Just as the scientific spirit digs the ground from beneath superstition, so does its fellow-worker, realism, tend to prick the bubble of abstract types. Realism is the tool of the democratic spirit, the modern spirit." [48] Such a writer as Howells, Perry pointed out, does not care for conventions: "What he cares for is to see and describe things as they are." [49]

Perry found that the realistic novel was the means by which modern literature might fulfill its evolutionary potential. It was the modern equivalent of Greek tragedy—a genre which was truthfully reflecting the conditions and ideals of contemporary life. In modern poetry "those men who have endeavored to establish a closer connection between life and letters have been lost sight of in the praise poured out on their more eloquent rivals." [50] But the novel as it developed "kept closer to the life of the time" and therefore "grew to be the most important expression of modern literature." [51] As practiced by Turgenev and Tolstoy, by certain French, Italian, and Spanish novelists, as well as by "the more eminent American novelists," [52] modern fiction was encouraging all literature "to break away from conventions . . . and see and portray life." [53] By means of the modern realistic novel the fluctuating history of literature since the Greeks might be replaced by a steady progress, since we have "begun again to see that life itself is something greater, vaster, and more solemn than any literary method." [54]

iv

Perry's reviews of the 1870's and his critical works of the 1880's were opposite sides of the same coin. In his reviews he supported realism, for—like evolution itself—there was nothing terrible in it; it was simply the contemporary product of the growth of literature and society. In his criticism he described the history of this growth and the forces which impeded it. His reiteration of the principle of growth was his conscious attempt to play some part in encouraging an acceptance of the priority of universal law over literary convention.

Using one of Perry's own critical beliefs, one can see that his practice of criticism was to a large extent conditioned and limited by his age. For though the contemporary enthusiasm for the use of evolutionary ideas in literary criticism had a number of salutary effects, it also contained several fallacies. Perry's work, for example, reveals one of the most attractive qualities of evolutionary criticism—a receptiveness to contemporary innovation and experimentation, whatever their unconventionality. It also reveals an awareness of the role of social forces in literature and of the importance of comparative studies.

Perhaps the greatest weakness in Perry's criticism is his establishment of goals for literature. Most nineteenth-century evolutionary philosophers (Spencer, for example) interpreted evolution as a progress toward certain social and ethical ends, and this tendency is apparent in evolutionary literary criticism as well. The paradox, of course, is that though evolutionary philosophers and critics viewed all life as mutable, they established immutable goals for social and literary evolution, goals which were derived primarily from nineteenth-century conditions and beliefs.[55] Perry's literary goals—nondidacticism and an exact social realism—are of this character.

In all, Perry's criticism of the 1880's embodies many of the advantages and pitfalls of the late nineteenth-century application of the theory of evolution to literary criticism. A refreshing willingness to view the artist as somewhat less than infallible, a realization of the social bases of art, and a partisan interest in the new are vitiated by a rigid formula to which all literature must conform and a conception of literary history as a progress toward contemporaneously conditioned literary goals.

6 EVOLUTIONARY CRITICISM AND THE DEFENSE OF HOWELLSIAN REALISM

TO THE GENERATION after Darwin the use of evolutionary ideas in the study of every phase of man's past appeared necessary for the attainment of truth. Broadly speaking, the theory of evolution helped bring about two important shifts of emphasis in historical studies. The discovery that species were not immutable played an important role in the nineteenth-century intellectual reorientation from an evaluative absolutism to a descriptive relativism. And the Darwinian stress upon environmental determinism aided in the shift of historical focus from the individual to his age's social milieu.[1] Many late nineteenth-century literary critics realized the significance of evolutionary ideas for the study of literature, and there was a pervasive and frequently acknowledged "Application of Evolutionary Principles to Art and Literature."[2] An excellent opportunity for the study of this application within the context of the rise of realism in America exists in the Boston literary scene of the 1880's, when three writers employed evolutionary ideas in their criticism in order to defend the work of W. D. Howells.

ii

Hamlin Garland, Thomas Sergeant Perry, George Pellew, and William Dean Howells experienced that sharing of ideas and enthusiasms within a particular locality which often results in a literary movement. Of the four, Howells and Perry had known each other since 1869, when Howells, the assistant editor of the *Atlantic Monthly*, had engaged Perry as a reviewer of foreign literature. They maintained a close literary and personal friendship for the rest of their lives.[3] Pellew had been a pupil of Perry's during the latter's tenure as a Harvard instructor of English in the late 1870's.[4] After several years of law practice in Boston, Pellew adopted a literary career, writing a life of John Jay (published 1890), and contributing poetry and critical articles to various magazines and newspapers.[5] Through Perry he came to know Howells, who considered him "a very able fellow, and distinctly a literary promise." [6] Garland, who arrived in Boston in 1884, became acquainted with Howells in 1887, with Pellew early the following year, and with Perry in 1889, shortly after Perry's return from two years abroad.[7]

During the 1880's Garland, Perry, and Pellew frequently directed their literary criticism toward a defense of Howellsian realism. Perhaps the opening statement in this defense was Perry's 1882 *Century* article on Howells, the terminal summation (as the writers dispersed to other cities or followed new interests) Garland's 1890 *New England Magazine* vindication of Howells's work. Between these dates Perry and Pellew published several works of literary history in which they often digressed to praise contemporary realism on evolutionary grounds. The attack which greeted Howells's advocacy of realism in his "Editor's Study" columns drew Garland and Pellew into explicit rejoinder during the closing years of the decade. Garland supported Howells in reviews, articles, and lectures.[8] Pellew contributed a widely noted defense of

Howells in a letter to the *Boston Post* in early 1888,[9] and continued to voice his approbation of Howellsian realism in critical articles.

The conception held in a common by Garland, Perry, and Pellew was that man's history revealed his continuous physical, social, and intellectual growth and development. The universality of the law of growth encouraged a belief in the unity of life. Literature was an intrinsic part of life, they believed, not something above or beyond it, and was governed by the same natural laws as any other aspect of life. The literary history of an era was understandable only in terms of literature's participation in the totality of life and therefore literature's reflection of the particular conditions of life of a particular era. The crucial point was that an age's literature could not be understood, and was not to be evaluated, on the basis of rules, standards, and conventions established in any other age, since these criteria reflected differing social and intellectual conditions. The use of critical standards derived from the past to judge contemporary literature was particularly disastrous, the three writers agreed, since all—from Garland fervently to Perry hesitantly—affirmed that change was progressive. In short, the three writers asserted a historical relativism which demanded that modern art be interpreted and judged on the basis of its truthful representation of contemporary life rather than its conformity to criteria which the universal law of progressive change had rendered obsolete and retrogressive. Their defense of Howellsian realism was based on their belief that it exhibited a freedom from past and a fidelity to present life. Each of the writers was fulfilling Garland's demand that criticism applaud literature which was "adaptive" and attack that which was "ancestral." [10]

iii

Out of his reading in Taine, Herbert Spencer, and H. M. Posnett, Hamlin Garland had constructed an evolutionary critical system which he expressed in his unpublished "The Evolution of American Thought" (written 1886–87), in numerous reviews and articles of the late eighties and early nineties, and in *Crumbling Idols* (1894). He stated in "The Evolution of American Thought": "Nothing is stable, nothing absolute, all changes, all is relative. Poetry, painting, the drama, these too are always being modified or left behind by the changes in society from which they spring." Since this was true, and since "the history of intellectual America for the last century is a history of the growth and dominance of ideas born of democratic social conditions," American literature should reflect the democratic life and ideals of modern America. Garland asserted this need despite the fact that "most of our poets, artists, and scholars have united themselves to the conservative, aristocratic element of the old world, measuring themselves—not by the approbation of democracy, not by reality—but by the classic models. . . . They [have] studied books and not men, the past and not the present." [11]

Garland's defense of Howells was based upon this evolutionary conception of literature. In his *New England Magazine* essay "Mr. Howells's Latest Novels," he refuted the contemporary critical attack on Howells's fiction by noting that

Criticism of Mr. Howells, with previous writers or living writers as criteria, has no value. He can be criticized properly in but one way—by comparison with life. Is he true? is the question to be asked. If he is false to his subject or to himself, then objections are valid. But to say that he is not Scott, or Dickens, or Hugo, or Dumas is certainly true, but it is not criticism. That he is different is a merit and a distinction, not, surely, because Scott and Dickens were not great, but because they no longer represent us. Art, in its progress, refuses to be held accountable to the past. It claims for itself the right to depict in its own way, its own time, just as its predecessors did.

As a critic, Mr. Howells may be said to represent the idea of progress in ideals. He stands over against the idea of the statical in art and literature.[12]

Garland closed his essay with a plea for the extension of such criticism, for

Only when the development of literature and art, the incessant change of ideals from age to age, is recognized . . . can full justice be done to the group of young writers now rising in America, who represent this new tendency and of whom Mr. Howells is the champion and the unquestioned leader.[13]

Thomas Sergeant Perry had already answered Garland's call for a critic aware of the need for historical relativism. During the late 1860's and early 1870's he had been influenced by John Fiske and other evolutionary writers and has espoused evolution as a theory applicable to literary study and criticism. His evolutionary critical beliefs led him to introduce and champion European realism in reviews and articles of the 1870's. And in the 1880's he expressed the theoretical foundation of his endorsement of realism in a series of works of literary criticism.

In 1882 Perry wrote of the application of evolutionary ideas to literature that "it's magnificent to have a principle abt. wh. things arrange themselves." [14] As interpreted by Perry, the primary characteristic of this principle was growth. There was nothing "terrible" in evolution, he assured a friend, "it is merely the hypothesis that everything is a matter of *growth*, as opposed to the notion of special creations." [15] The "everything" in Perry's definition of course included literature, and the function of the modern critic was therefore the "scientific examination . . . of historical growth." [16] Such an examination inevitably revealed that writers were not inexplicable miracles, but rather participants in a universal process of social and literary development. Every writer, Perry argued,

> is bound by the necessity of building on the foundations that society is laying every day . . . and is limited by experience whether this be treated literally or be modified by the imagination. No writer can escape this limitation any more than he can imagine a sixth sense. If these statements are accurate, and a general, although not uniform, progress is acknowledged to exist in society, literature may also be said to be under the sway of law, or, rather, to move in accordance with law.[17]

Much of Perry's work in literary history was directed toward indicating that throughout the history of literature few writers or critics had been aware of literature's participation in the law of progressive change. There had been insufficient recognition of the intrinsic relationship between literature and life and of the dependence of literature upon life for its strength and growth. This failure had resulted in such deserts of literary history as the eighteenth century, when life was ignored for a "formal correctness" based on Latin models.[18] But "what is best in all literature," Perry declared, "is the most natural form of expression, a form that grows from the soil." [19] Greek literature, for example, owed its greatness to its close relationship to Greek life and its freedom from literary conventions. "Of no people is it truer than of the Greeks," Perry wrote, "that their literature is not an artificial product, but the race speaking. The most important thing to remember in studying their writings is that these are the direct expression of a free people, leading its own life, untrammeled by inherited rules or authoritative convention." [20] With the Greeks, "literature was, as it should be, as broad as life itself; belief and doubt, joy and sorrow, enthusiasm and contempt, all found natural expression without reference to a literary code." [21]

Perry championed modern realism because it was attempting to return literature to the directness, naturalness, and freedom from authority which were the sources of literature's participation in evolutionary progress. By means of the realistic novel the fluctuating history of literature might be replaced by a steady progress, for writers had "begun again to see that life itself is something greater, vaster, and more solemn than any literary method." [22] Realism, which incorporated the reaction against authority encouraged by the rise of science and democracy, was endeavoring to portray life with the fidelity to contemporary experience and disregard for past conventions characteristic of Greek tragedy. In his *Century* article on Howells, Perry placed Howells in the forefront of this attempt:

> After all, what can realism produce but the downfall of conventionality? Just as the scientific spirit digs the ground from beneath superstition, so does its fellow-worker, realism, tend to prick the bubble of abstract types. Realism is the tool of the democratic spirit, the modern spirit by means of which the truth is elicited, and Mr. Howells' realism is untiring.[23]

Howells "does not care for conventions," Perry concluded. "What he cares for is to see and describe things as they are . . . ." [24]

In early 1888, when George Pellew learned of Garland's admiration for Howells's work, he wrote Garland that "it was a delightful surprise to find that there were others in Boston who were not arrayed against

Mr. Howells." Pellew went on to note that he was "a friend of T. S. Perry and owe to him most of what little knowledge of letters I possess . . . ." [25] This debt is clearly evident in Pellew's *Jane Austen's Novels,* which opens with an attack on critics who characterize Jane Austen as inexplicably unique:

> They speak of her, as men often speak of Burns, as a singular and inexplicable phenomenon, without connection with the past. But such independence is impossible, even for a poet or a novelist. In natural history, in the history of institutions or in that of fiction, the same laws hold true,—that in time every thing changes, and that this change is not from nothing into something, but by growth from what existed before, or by reaction against it. [26]

Pellew therefore examined Jane Austen as a product of the contemporary state of development of her society and of the novel. He found her limited by the immaturity of both, despite her wit and charm. She was distinguished, however, by her "faculty of describing accurately what she saw," which "anticipated the scientific precision that the spirit of the age is now demanding in literature and art." [27] He pointed out that although this faculty had had an obstructed development, "we may believe that the art and fiction of the future will gradually be brought into ever closer relation to the facts of experience." [28]

In his article on "The New Battle of the Books," Pellew observed that any return to romanticism was retrogressive, since society and man had progressed beyond the social conditions and the level of knowledge which had produced romanticism:

> In the beginning of the century the influence of heredity and the dependence of the individual character upon the social environment were not understood. An honest return, therefore, to the point of view of the early

romanticists [that is, to the romantic hero] is now impossible, and such novels as they wrote cannot be written now without affectation. Human sympathy has broadened, society has become more democratic; a scientific study of history has shown the interdependence of all men, the comparative unimportance of exceptional men, and the all-importance of those commonplace individuals who form the mass of a people . . . . [29]

Realism, on the other hand, Pellew explained in his 1891 article summarizing "Ten Years of American Literature," embodied the concern for both science and democracy characteristic of the contemporary state of development. "Democracy," he wrote, "as it has become self-conscious, has felt ever-increasing interest in familiar human life and familiar scenes," and "the scientific spirit of the age has popularized the love of accurate descriptions, of 'human documents.' " [30] Howells, he noted, was the acknowledged leader of the realistic movement, and Howells and Perry were the only "scientific" critics in America. [31]

It was such a belief that had prompted Pellew's vigorous defense of Howells in the *Boston Post* early in 1888, a defense which Howells characterized as "a most generous thing . . . [which] really turned the tide of contumely, in several places." [32] Pellew began by recalling that "for about two years there has hardly been a single issue of any Boston paper which has not contained some defamatory personal reference to Mr. Howells and his novels." But in what way had Howells offended in his fiction and criticism, Pellew inquired. He replied:

Simply in adopting a theory of literary criticism that is in closer agreement with the scientific method than the personal criticism that reflects chiefly the likes and dislikes of the critics. He believes that the principles of evolution apply to literature as they apply to government and art, and in so believing he is in accord with the best recent work in Germany, France, and Italy. He perceives that in the history of fiction there has been a gradual change from the incoherent fancies of dreams towards correspondence with the veracities of waking life.[33]

Howells's realization of the growth of "the power of accurate representation," and his willingness to write and judge fiction on the basis of "a reference to experience," were grounds for praise, Pellew concluded, rather than vilification.[34]

iv

The importance of the defense of Howells by Garland, Perry, and Pellew is that it reveals something about the intellectual foundations of the advocacy and defense of realism in late nineteenth-century America. The three writers believed that realism was a mode of viewing life which incorporated the two great wonders of nineteenth-century America—the material advances of science and the individual opportunity and freedom of democracy. The theory of evolutionary progress served as an inclusive formula for linking and endorsing science, democracy, and realism. Just as social and intellectual progress had resulted in democracy and the rise of science, so literary progress had produced realism, which embodied the ideals of democracy and the methodology of science. It was with a firm belief that their defense of realism was also a defense of both natural law and American ideals that Garland, Perry, and Pellew spoke out with vigor and indignation on behalf of Howells.

7 EVOLUTIONARY IDEAS IN LATE NINETEENTH-CENTURY ENGLISH AND AMERICAN LITERARY CRITICISM

AS WE ENTER the second century of *The Origin of Species* we recognize that the theory of evolution is one of the dominant ideas of recent history and that we have just begun to explore its impact on the world of ideas beyond its manifestation in controversies between science and religion. I would like to offer a sketch of the influence of evolutionary ideas on one portion of that world, that of late nineteenth-century literary criticism in English. I will first outline briefly the various stages of this influence, and then discuss the particular ways in which evolutionary ideas contributed to the modification of the study and evaluation of literature in America and England during the last three decades of the century.

It is possible to distinguish three roughly chronological periods in the influence of evolutionary ideas. First, during the 1870's and 1880's certain critics whose thought and values were essentially pre-Darwinian drew upon evolutionary ideas to support preconceived critical and ethical positions. Such writers as Sidney Lanier and E. C. Stedman, for example, paid little heed to the materialistic and deterministic implications of evolutionary science. Rather, they responded to the individualism and optimism of Spencerian evolution and adapted selected portions of evolutionary thought to confirm romantic conceptions of the purpose and value of literature. During the 1880's and 1890's, on the other hand, a number of critics drew more deeply upon evolutionary ideas. Thomas Sergeant Perry, Hamlin Garland, William Morton Payne, John Addington Symonds, and H. M. Posnett relied upon the historical relativism and environmental determinism implicit in the ideas of evolution, and also upon Herbert Spencer's master evolutionary formula, in their attempts to construct fully elaborated evolutionary systems. The last period in the influence of evolutionary ideas began in the 1880's and still continues. Academic critics such as Brander Matthews, H. H. Boyesen, and Edward Dowden, as well as such professional literary men as William Dean Howells and George Pellew, did not go to the extreme of building evolutionary critical systems. Rather, they absorbed into their critical practices and beliefs certain by-products of the evolutionary conception of the nature of literature and the function of the critic. The weary graduate student who today has to read Boileau along with Dryden, who complains of lengthy reading lists consisting of minor works by minor figures, who has to know Trevelyan's *Social History* as well as Baugh's *Literary History*, little realizes that he is at least in part engaged in "the scientific study of literature" as many evolutionary critics of the late nineteenth century conceived of that study.

Evolutionary ideas influenced the study and evaluation of literature in three ways during the late nineteenth century. First, the widely held conviction that the principles of evolution evident in man's biological past could also be found in his intellectual and social past encouraged a belief that literature grew and changed according to natural law—that literature, like life, was dynamic rather than static, and that its condition at any one moment of time could be understood only by an examination of its development from its previous condition. Secondly, evolutionary ideas supported an emphasis on the milieu as the determining factor in literary production rather than the individual writer. It was the literary and social environment which conditioned the writer's ideals, material, and methods and which therefore ultimately determined the pattern of literary history. Lastly, evolutionary studies fostered a conception of the critic or historian as an analogue to the scientist—as an analytical observer and codifier of literary specimens rather than a belletristic entertainer or an arbitrary determiner of value.

Let me examine each of these major patterns of influence in greater detail. The concept of change is fundamental to evolutionary thought, and Darwin's belief that biological change is the product of variation and natural selection was immediately available as a possible means of examining change in other phases of man's experience. The application to literary study of the environmental determinism implicit in the theory of natural selection was also encouraged, of course, by Taine's belief that literature is the product of a nation's physical and social conditions. But the basic pattern of evolutionary change which was joined to Taine's environmental determinism to produce an evolutionary critical system was seldom Darwinian. Rather, most critics accepted and absorbed Herbert Spencer's doctrine that evolution is, in all phases of life, a progress from the simplicity of incoherent homogeneity to the complexity of coherent heterogeneity. There were several reasons why the Spencerian formula appealed to literary men. It was universally applicable, explicitly optimistic, and easily grasped; it was capable of wide variation depending on the predilections of the individual writer; and, perhaps most of all as far as American criticism was concerned, it permitted the critic to view the history of literature as a progress toward a democratic individualism in expression and subject matter.[1]

The combination of Taine and Spencer is therefore the basic pattern in most evolutionary critical systems of the 1880's and 1890's. A typical example is H. M. Posnett's juxtaposition of the static and the dynamic. Posnett argued that the critic must organize his studies

> round certain central facts of comparatively permanent influence. Such facts are the climate, soil, animal and plant life of different countries; such also is the principle of evolution from communal [that is, homogeneous] to individual [that is, heterogeneous] life. . . . The former may be called the statical influences to which literature has been everywhere exposed; the latter may be called the dynamical principle of literature's progress and decay.[2]

What Posnett called the dynamic, T. S. Perry named growth and J. A. Symonds process. "The fundamental conception which underlies the Evolutionary method of thought," Symonds explained, "is that all things in the universe exist in process. No other system has so vigorously enforced the truth that it is impossible to isolate phenomena from their antecedents and their consequents."[3] Like Posnett, Symonds viewed change in Spencerian terms. "Evolution," he stated, "may be defined as the passage of all things, inorganic and organic, by the action of inevitable law, from simplicity to complexity, from an undifferentiated to a differentiated condition."[4] The belief that literature was largely a product of social conditions, and that these

conditions changed according to the Spencerian formula, is exemplified by Hamlin Garland's unpublished
"The Evolution of American Thought." In this work,
written during 1886–87, Garland explained that the
progress of American literature was dependent upon
the growth of heterogeneity in American social and
intellectual life.[5] The application of the Spencerian
formula is also illustrated by Posnett's organization of
the history of European literature around the progress
from the clan to the city-state to the nation to the
individual,[6] and by T. S. Perry's conception of the
history of the drama. Perry wrote:

> The change from a drama that represented only kings
> and heroes of princely birth to one that concerned itself
> with human beings, was as inevitable a thing as is the
> change in government from despotism to democracy,
> with the growth of the importance of the individual.
> There is a certain monotony in civilization which may
> be exemplified in a thousand ways. The large gas pipes,
> for instance, that are laid in every street, and then have
> the smaller branches running into every house, which
> again feed the ramifying tubes that supply the single
> lights, may remind one of the advance from the general
> to the particular which characterizes every form of
> human thought.[7]

But whatever the degree of Spencerianism in particular critics, the primary characteristics of evolutionary
criticism were adequately summarized by William
Morton Payne when he wrote, "We are coming to
understand more and more clearly that . . . the history of literature is the history of a process, and the
study of a work of literature is the study of a product.
To this, in the last analysis, the evolutionary conception of literature reduces." [8] Hamlin Garland was even
more explicit when he stated that "Nothing is stable,

nothing absolute, all changes, all is relative. Poetry, painting, the drama, these too are always being modified or left behind by the changes in society from which they spring." [9]

The dynamic quality of literature was not only the result of literature's intrinsic relationship with a society continually in flux. Literature also contained within itself a constantly changing element, one comparable to a species in biological life. Like a species, a literary genre pursued a life cycle from birth to maturity to death and decay. Explanations of the cause of this cycle differed somewhat from critic to critic. William Morton Payne believed that there was a struggle for existence among genres. [10] Symonds and Perry held that the works within a genre inevitably reached a high point, after which they substituted literary imitation for a reflection of life, a failure to adapt to environment which ultimately caused the decline of the genre. [11] The important similarity among all critics employing a genre approach to the evolution of literature was their belief in the subservience of the individual writer to the stage of development of his genre. Writers in the "stone age" of fiction, Howells observed, such as Scott and Balzac, were not to be blamed for their flaws in technique and content. [12] Even Goethe in his fiction could not rise above the low development of the novel during his age. "What is useful in any review of Goethe's methods," Howells wrote, "is the recognition of the fact . . . that the greatest master cannot produce a masterpiece in a new kind. The novel was too recently invented in Goethe's day not to be, even in his hands, full of the faults of apprentice work." [13] T. S. Perry, on the other hand, pointed out that praise was usually unjustified for a later writer in a genre on the basis of his superiority to an earlier. Sophocles reached a greater height than

Aeschylus, Perry noted, but he then went on to explain that the difference between them "was not so much a personal one as it was the necessary result of their relative positions in the history of the Greek drama." [14]

The effect of the application to literary study of both the Spencerian conception of progress and the conception of the genre as analogous to a species was to diminish the importance of the author in literary creation. In this tendency evolutionary critics locked horns with the romantic celebration of genius. Many evolutionary critics openly attacked the idea that the genius was above or outside law. They pointed out that the reliance upon an inexplicable outburst of genius as an explanation of literary production was comparable to the reliance placed upon special creation in the explanation of biological existence. T. S. Perry complained that although the idea that it is possible to evoke "something out of nothing by direct exercise of creative power . . . has vanished from science, it still survives in those departments of human activity which have not yet come fully under scientific treatment, and poets and painters enjoy in the popular estimation a privilege which has been denied to nature." [15] The cult of genius was a "mischievous superstition," as Howells put it,[16] which hindered the realization that all writers, whatever their degree of ability, were dependent upon their time and place for inspiration and material.

Of course, most evolutionary critics recognized the existence of literary greatness, a phenomenon which they explained variously as either the result of one extreme in the spectrum of literary ability, or as the literary parallel of "spontaneous variations"—that is, biological sports.[17] Hamlin Garland expressed a typical conception of the interplay between the writer and his milieu when he noted that:

> In evolution there are always two vast fundamental forces; one, the inner, which propels; the other, the outer, which adapts and checks. One forever thrusts toward new forms, the other forever moulds, conserves, adapts, reproduces. . . . The force that flowers is the individual, that which checks and moulds is environment.[18]

But in their reaction against the prevalent "great man" school of historical and critical writing, most evolutionary critics tended to emphasize the outer force. Symonds reflected this tendency when he wrote, "The Evolutionist differs from previous students mainly in this, that he regards the totality of the phenomena presented as something necessitated by conditions to which the prime agents in the process, Marlowe or even Shakespeare, were subordinated." [19] In short, evolutionary criticism posited a literature of law, not men.

The evolutionary critics believed that criticism had reached a high point in the modern period. Perhaps the most influential depiction of the advance of criticism was that of Symonds, who viewed the critic as progressively judge, showman, and scientist, or, in another context, as classicist, romanticist, and scientist.[20] Whatever tags they applied to earlier criticism, however, all evolutionary critics used the term scientific to designate the modern critic who, like the scientist, sought a truthful description of the phenomenon under study, a description which precluded exhibitionism and judgment. Howells cautioned that the function of the modern critic was "to classify and analyze the fruits of the human mind very much as the naturalist classifies the objects of his study, rather than to praise or blame them," [21] while Perry suggested that "it is a question whether praise and blame, admiration and contempt, have anything whatsoever to do with literary history. Our sole aim should be to know . . . ."[22] In practice, however, despite Dowden's early and influential call for historical relativism in criticism,[23] most evolutionary critics did apply evaluative standards. They believed that literature progressed as the whole of life progressed, and that the best work of art was therefore almost always that which most closely mirrored the social and intellectual life of its time. In other words, literature was not only describable in terms of its close relation to life, but could also be judged on the basis of its varying degree of reflection of that life. It was this characteristic of evolutionary criticism which made most American evolutionary critics such staunch supporters of realism during the literary controversies of the 1880's and 1890's.

Nevertheless, in theory the scientific critic was distinguished by a willingness to discard judgment and to view literature as a historical process. William Morton Payne called such a critic a "natural historian" of literature and described him as one who

> endeavors primarily to account for the work, to view it with reference to the conditions that have attended its production, to consider it, sometimes as a natural development in an established line, sometimes as the expression of a new tendency born of a changed environment or a fresh impulse given the human intellect. . . . He looks before and after, and views literary productions as members of a system rather than as sporadic appearances, as links in a causal chain rather than as isolated phenomena.[24]

Scientific criticism, Payne concluded, is that "controlled by the doctrine of evolution as a guiding principle."[25]

The comparative method, which Posnett characterized as "the great glory" of nineteenth-century thought,[26] was one of the primary tools of the evolutionary critic as well as the evolutionary scientist. It was Darwin's ability to note the similarities and dissimilarities among a large number of species of various areas which had led to his great discovery. Payne indicated the pervasiveness of the association of the comparative method with evolutionary criticism when he claimed that

> The study of literature in the evolutionary sense tends more and more to become a comparative study. Just as the geological series of deposits, confused or abruptly broken off in one country, may be found continued elsewhere, so some line of development among the *genres* of literature, clear up to a certain point in the product of one nation, may from that point on be better traced by transferring the scrutiny to some other field.[27]

A possible approach to the understanding and evaluation of evolutionary criticism is to adopt Payne's critical dictum that the critic must look "before and after." Like many literary movements, evolutionary criticism began in reaction, in this case reaction against the supposed subjectivism and absolutism of the criticism of the previous age. It wished to replace personal willfulness and outworn conventions with the law of evolution, an undertaking which to many in the generation after Darwin appeared to be necessary for the attainment of truth in all phases of life. Of course, in their enthusiasm most evolutionary critics went too far, particularly in their attempts to find biological analogues in literature, in the rigid determinism of their conception of literary change, and in their diminution of the aesthetic evaluative functions of the critic. But looking "after" as well as "before," one can see that the movement was part of a larger reorientation in man's examination of his cultural past, and that it served as a now discarded prelude to much that is accepted and valued in modern criticism and research. It confirmed, for example, the beliefs that discernible change is a major condition of literary history, that an understanding of the life and conventions of a particular age is important and necessary for the understanding of works written during that age, and that comparative studies are a significant contribution to literary research.[28] As in almost every aspect of thought it touched, the theory of evolution aided in the modification of our ideas—in this instance, those concerning the nature and the proper study of literature.

8 HAMLIN GARLAND
AND STEPHEN CRANE:
THE NATURALIST AS
ROMANTIC INDIVIDUALIST

MOST CRITICS of American literature no longer feel
obliged, as did Bliss Perry in 1912, to preface an
examination of the American mind with a defense of
the attempt.[1] Now accepted are the beliefs that the
American experience has been unique and that it has
resulted in both a unique intellectual consciousness
known as the American mind and a unique literature.
What is less certain, however, is the particular nature
of the American experience and mind and of their
effect upon American literature. One of the most
striking common denominators in otherwise often diverse interpretations of the American mind is that of
romantic individualism—that is, a pervasive and widespread faith in the validity of the individual experience
and mind as a source of knowledge and a guide to
action. It is true, of course, that this romantic individualism has never lacked criticism. But its tenacious
strength in spite of frequently valid and forceful attack
is itself an indication of the depth of the faith in the
individual in American life, whether it be expressed in
Jeffersonian liberalism, transcendentalism, or the literary revolt of the twenties.
    I would like to examine the nature and scope of

romantic individualism in the critical ideas of Hamlin Garland and Stephen Crane. These two writers are often discussed as naturalists, and the period in which they flourished is almost always considered primarily as a segment of the European naturalistic movement and its influence and manifestation in America. The Zola-esque experimental method is explained and the use of such "scientific" elements in literature as the force of heredity and environment is sketched. All this, of course, is pertinent and necessary. But it is also necessary to indicate that the early American naturalists were very much nineteenth-century Americans and that much in their work and ideas which makes them square pegs in the round hole of such a "standard" definition of naturalism as "pessimistic determinism" may be caused by their absorption of nineteenth-century American ideas. For though Garland and Crane are usually (and rightfully) considered to be among the earliest representatives of American literary naturalism, I wish to point out in addition—not that they were at heart Jeffersonians, transcendentalists, or anticipators of the twenties—but rather that they too, each in his own way, consciously and unconsciously, were part of the broad current which is the stream of American romantic individualism.

ii

In his introduction to *Crumbling Idols*, Hamlin Garland noted the twofold purpose of the work: "to weaken the hold of conventionalism upon the youthful artist" and "to be constructive, by its statement and insistent restatement that American art, to be enduring and worthy, must be original and creative, not imitative." [2] Both of these purposes were intrinsically linked to the evolutionary interpretation of literature Garland had derived during his early years in

Boston. During those years (1884–87) he had immersed himself first in the works of Taine and Herbert
Spencer and later in those of Edward Dowden, H. M.
Posnett, William Dean Howells, and Thomas Sergeant Perry. From Taine he accepted a belief that
literature was conditioned by time and place. From
Spencer, the source of much of his thought, Garland
formulated a conception of literature as a dynamic
phenomenon closely related to the physical and social
evolutionary progress from incoherent homogeneity to
coherent heterogeneity. With the aid of H. M.
Posnett's *Comparative Literature* he then combined
these two ideas into an evolutionary critical system.
Literature was required to keep pace with evolutionary
progress by mirroring the intense social and individual
differences which the progress from homogeneity to
heterogeneity had caused. He concluded that the local
colorist was the only writer capable of capturing contemporary social and individual complexity, since he
alone worked in close enough detail with an area he
knew intimately.

This "dynamic concept of art"—that is, the idea
that art must reflect an ever-changing world—Garland
first stated in an unpublished series of lectures, "The
Evolution of American Thought," and repeated again
and again in *Crumbling Idols*. "Life is always changing," he wrote, "and literature changes with it. It never
decays; it changes." [77] The relativist position in
artistic creation and criticism was that art is not a
matter of the imitation or use of the great works or
ideas of the past, but that "life is the model."

Garland, then, conceived of literature as his contem-
poraries in American philosophy, the pragmatists—also
founding their system upon evolutionary thought—
conceived of ideas.[3] Just as ideas were not absolute because they must work in the world and the world is ever

changing, so art has no absolutes, but must reflect and interpret an ever-changing world by means of new material and new forms. And just as William James's pragmatism sets up a pluralistic universe in which the individual is the source of truth, so Garland conceived of artistic truth as pluralistic and as centered in the individual artist.

Garland derived this emphasis on impressionistic artistic truth from his reading of Véron's *Aesthetics* shortly after he had formulated his evolutionary critical system. In his extensively marked and annotated copy of Véron he wrote on the first page of the Introduction: "This book influenced me more than any other work on art. It entered into all I thought and spoke and read for many years after it fell into my hands about 1886." [4] Véron's critical ideas appealed to Garland because they were in a number of ways parallel to those he himself had just formulated. In his opposition to the French Academy, Véron, who was also the author of *La supériorité des arts modernes sur les arts anciens*, was much in step with the contemporary ideas which had influenced Garland. He too claimed to be using science as the basis for his study, and he too demanded that the artist deal with life about him, since evolution "must give birth to new forms of art appropriate to the new forms of civilization." [5] But whereas Garland had required that local color be the means by which the artist keep pace with evolution, Véron required a form of impressionism. "There are but three ways open to art," he wrote, "the imitation of previous forms of art; the realistic imitation of actual things; the manifestation of individual impressions . . . ." Of these three forms of art, Véron argued that only the last deserved the name, for "the determinant and essential constituent of art, is the personality of the artist." [6] But it should be empha-

sized that Véron's impressionism was restricted and
controlled by his insistence that art be anchored in
observed fact: "TRUTH and PERSONALITY: these are the
alpha and omega of art formulas; *truth* as to facts, and
the *personality* of the artist." [7]

Here was a system which shared two characteristics
of Garland's own belief. It stressed the necessity for art
to represent change, and it required that this be done
through the expression of individual personality, the
most important product of evolutionary progress from
homogeneity to heterogeneity. Garland was sufficiently
impressed by Véron's ideas to begin using them almost
immediately. So, for example, in noting a talk with his
artist friend John Enneking in early 1887, Garland described Enneking's artistic principles in terms of
Véron's three kinds of art. Enneking had initially been
"conventional" and had "sought the ideal," Garland
noted. He had then turned to nature in an attempt to
depict it "absolutely as it was." His third and final
stage was comparable to Véron's personal impression
of observed fact. "He now paints the effect of a scene.
That is, he gives us the natural as it affects him." [8]

Garland had little difficulty placing Véron within
his evolutionary critical system, since an individual
response to observed fact was but another way, to
Garland, of stating the idea of local color and all its
implications for American literature. For the only
literature which could reflect truthfully the life of a
particular time and place was that produced by the
individual artist, unshackled by rules and conventions,
working in close harmony to that life. Garland wrote
in *Crumbling Idols*:

Art, I must insist, is an individual thing,—the question
of one man facing certain facts and telling his individual
relations to them. His first care must be to present his
own concept. This is, I believe, the essence of veritism:

"Write of those things of which you know most, and for which you care most. By so doing you will be true to yourself, true to your locality, and true to your time." [35]

But as Garland pointed out in *Crumbling Idols*, "The sun of truth strikes each part of the earth at a little different angle . . . ." [22] As truth is relative in time because of evolutionary change, so it is relative in place owing to the product of that change, the increased social complexity and heightened individuality which have resulted from evolutionary progress. The impressionist or veritist reflecting the life around him cannot help being a local colorist, since by his reference to nature he must needs represent the uniqueness of his particular area. In *Crumbling Idols* Garland stated an aesthetic system in which evolutionary ideas served as the intellectual foundation, impressionism as the artistic method advocated, and local color as the end product in the various arts.

Throughout *Crumbling Idols* Garland used *impressionism* and *veritism* interchangeably. For example, he defined the two in almost exactly similar terms. Impressionism was "the statement of one's individual perception of life and nature, guided by devotion to truth" [50]; while "This *theory* of the veritist is, after all, a statement of his passion for truth and for individual expression." [21] He appears to have derived the coined word *veritism* as an antonym for *effectism*, Valdés's term (popularized by Howells) for the sensational in literature. In an early article on Ibsen, Garland praised Ibsen's handling of character because it followed "the general principle of verity first and effect afterwards," [9] and later in the same discussion he used the word *veritist* for the first time. But for Garland, "true" art was primarily the product of an individual response to observed fact, and the term *veritist* soon received the impressionistic cast with which it is used in *Crumbling Idols*.

Far from being the awkward yawp of a confused naturalist (as it usually has been considered), *Crumbling Idols* embodies a coherent aesthetic system. Central to this system—and the emotional center of reference in all of Garland's thought—was the right and need of the individual to be free. The artist must be freed from past and present literary masters in order that he may perceive for himself the truth of his own locality and thereby keep literature in step with evolutionary progress. As Emerson had attempted to free the American scholar from that which prevented him from perceiving truth for himself and had called for men of letters to throw off the domination of Europe, so Garland called upon the young writer of the West to interpret life for himself and cast off his subservience to the East. And even Emerson and Whitman—those fountainheads of American radical individualism—would not have stated the doctrine of faith in the individual artist more vigorously than Garland at the close of *Crumbling Idols*:

> Rise, O young man and woman of America! Stand erect! Face the future with a song on your lips and the light of a broader day in your eyes. Turn your back on the past, not in scorn, but in justice to the future. Cease trying to be correct, and become creative. This is our day. The past is not vital. . . .To know Shakespeare is good. To know your fellowmen is better. All that Shakespeare knew of human life, you may know, but not at second hand, not through Shakespeare, not through the eyes of the dead, but at first hand. [190–91] [10]

iii

For the past thirty years or more it has been customary to begin any consideration of Stephen

Crane with an account of the critical neglect of his work. This complaint is no longer justified, for there has been of late much critical interest in both Crane's biography and his work. From the initial treatment of Crane as an inexplicable genius, as a literary "natural," there has evolved a conception of him as a conscious and subtle craftsman and artist. From being considered as a bright but short-lived and uninfluential meteor in the literary firmament, he is now thought, somewhat exaggeratedly to be sure, to have innovated the "two main technical movements of modern fiction—realism and symbolism." [11]

My concern here, however, is not with the meaning or technique of Crane's writing, but rather with the quality of mind and literary self-confidence which led him to that writing. This self-confidence took two literary forms—a choice of material which would shock, as in *Maggie* (1893); and a willingness to trust his imagination in dealing with material about which he knew little, as in *The Red Badge of Courage* (1895). The story of a prostitute who was both a product and a victim of her environment was perhaps not as contemporaneously shocking as it was once thought to be, but to Crane, a young and comparatively unread writer, it appeared so. [12] He inscribed several copies of *Maggie* with the admonition that "It is inevitable that you will be greatly shocked by the book but continue, please, with all possible courage, to the end." [13] A serious author who will knowingly shock his readers is an author confident of the correctness of his vision of life, despite its being out of joint with conventional morality. And an author who will—as Crane did in *The Red Badge*—trust his imaginative conception of war and of its effects on men is just as confident of the validity of his personal vision.

One reason for Crane's self-confidence suggests itself immediately. Both *Maggie* and *The Red Badge* were written before Crane was twenty-three. In Crane's case, however, the self-confidence of a youthful and temperamentally cocky personality was reinforced and given an explicit rhetoric by the acceptance of an impressionistic critical doctrine. A clue to the source of this doctrine lies in Crane's lifelong sense of debt toward Hamlin Garland and William Dean Howells. This sense of debt was undoubtedly derived in part from Garland's and Howells's early aiding and championing of Crane. But it also derived, it appears, from Crane's early adoption and use of a particular critical idea of Garland's and Howells's.

In 1891, when Crane was nineteen and had as yet written little, he spent the summer helping his brother report New Jersey shore news for the *New York Tribune*. One of his assignments was to cover a series of "Lecture Studies in American Literature and Expressive Art" which Hamlin Garland was giving at the Avon-by-the-Sea Seaside Assembly.[14] Garland, at this time, was an enthusiastic advocate of impressionism in painting and literature and was formulating and writing the essays which would comprise *Crumbling Idols*. On August 17, Garland gave a lecture on Howells which Crane reported for the *Tribune*. Garland, in discussing Howells's work and ideas, placed him squarely in his own evolutionary, impressionistic critical system. Howells, Crane reported Garland, believed in " 'the progress of ideals, the relative in art.' " He therefore " 'does not insist upon any special material, but only that the novelist be true to himself and to things as he sees them.' " [15] On the surface, it would appear that these remarks would make little impression on a listener. But Crane not only heard them, he reported them. Moreover, he immediately became acquainted with Garland and spent some time with him

at Avon that summer and the next, when Garland
again gave a lecture series and Crane again reported
shore news.

In 1895 Crane inscribed a copy of *The Red Badge* to
Howells as a token of the "veneration and gratitude of
Stephen Crane for many things he has learned of the
common man and, above all, for a certain re-
adjustment of his point of view victoriously concluded
some time in 1892." [16] About a year earlier he had
written in a letter that in 1892 he had renounced the
"clever school in literature" and had "developed all
alone a little creed of art which I thought was a good
one. Later I discovered that my creed was identical
with the one of Howells and Garland . . . ." [17] The
important elements in these two statements of literary
indebtedness are Crane's realization of a debt to
Howells and his further realization of the similarity of
his "little creed" with the critical ideas of Garland and
Howells. Whether Crane discovered his creed "all
alone" and merely received confirmation from Garland and Howells, or whether he "victoriously concluded" his acceptance of the creed after being introduced to it by Garland's statement of Howells's belief,
is perhaps not too important. Important, rather, is
Crane's derivation in 1892 of a concept of personal
honesty and vision similar to both Garland's
idea—which Garland saw exemplified in Howells—
that "'the novelist [must] be true to himself and
to things as he sees them'" and Howells's own
statement that the novelist should above all "remember that there is no greatness, no beauty, which
does not come from truth to your own knowledge of
things." [18] Crane distinctly parallels these statements
in several of his sparsely recorded critical remarks. In
1896, for example, he wrote: "I had no other purpose
in writing 'Maggie' than to show people to people as

they seem to me. If that be evil, make the most of it." [19] Earlier that year he had stated this idea even more elaborately: ". . . I understand that a man is born into the world with his own pair of eyes, and he is not at all responsible for his vision—he is merely responsible for his quality of personal honesty." [20]

Crane, then, entered the literary arena armed with a powerful weapon—a belief in the primacy of his personal vision. On a superficial level, this faith led him to exploit and defend the unconventional and forbidden in *Maggie*, confident of the validity of showing "people to people as they seem to me." On a level of greater depth and significance, his faith in his own vision led him to exploit his inner eye, his imaginative conception of war and its effects. In both, Crane—like Garland—was revealing an acceptance of the strain of romantic individualism which demands that the artist above all be independent and self-reliant, that he be confident that within himself lies the touchstone of artistic truth.

9 THE SIGNIFICANCE OF FRANK NORRIS'S LITERARY CRITICISM

ALTHOUGH Frank Norris's critical essays are poorly written, repetitious, and occasionally plain silly, they nevertheless contain a coherent critical attitude of some importance. Norris is not often discussed as a writer capable of intellectual consistency in any matter. Most critics have approached him as did Franklin Walker in his biography of Norris. In that work Walker stressed Norris's boyish enthusiasm and his code of "feeling" raised above "thought." [1] Professor Walker implied by this emphasis that Norris was not a systematic thinker and that it would be futile to search for a consistent intellectual position in his fiction or criticism. But Walker's characterization of Norris is misleading for two reasons. A writer under thirty does not have to appear solemn to think seriously. And the rejection of "thought" for "feeling" is itself capable of expansion into an elaborate intellectual position. Because Norris advised others to feel does not mean that his advice was not reasoned. Indeed, in the history of man much thought has been devoted to the creation of anti-intellectual philosophies.

At the heart of the unified and coherent system of ideas underlying Norris's criticism is a primitivistic anti-intellectualism. [2] One method of describing this system is to adopt as convenient counter words the key terms in Norris's cry that life is better than literature. Superficially, he meant by this statement that first-hand experience ("life") is better than second-hand experience ("literature"). But when the terms are placed in the context of Norris's critical essays, one realizes that they are his inadequate symbols for two rich and opposing clusters of ideas and values. I therefore use "life" and "literature" both with a recognition of their deficiencies as generally viable critical terminology and with an appreciation of their usefulness and appropriateness when analysing Norris's critical ideas.

To Norris, "life" included the emotions and the instincts. It incorporated both the world of nature (the outdoors and the country) and the kind of life which Norris believed "natural" (the life of passion and violence, and the life of the low and fallen) because such life was closest to the primitive in man and furthest from the cultivated. "Literature," on the other hand, included thought, culture, overeducation, refinement, and excessive spirituality. "Life" was dominated by connotations of masculinity, naturalness, and strength; "literature" by suggestions of effeminacy, artificiality, and weakness. "Life" was the source of good art—from it sprang art which moved and led men—whereas from "literature" came imitative and affected art, written entirely for money or for the approval of a cult, or because the artist was unfortunate or unknowing enough to overrefine his temperament and to neglect the crude, raw, often violent world of action and affairs—the world of men and of nature. Norris thus made the emotional and instinctive the key to both the method and the material of fiction, since he encouraged writers to respond to a world of nonintellectuality with their own untaught vision.

Although primitivistic anti-intellectualism has a long history in American literature, Norris's expression of it differs from that of earlier and later writers with generally similar values. The central polarity in such writers as Hawthorne and Thoreau or Steinbeck and Faulkner is not only between the emotional-instinctive and the intellectual, but also, and more far-reaching, between the organicism of nature and the mechanization of science and industrialism. Norris, however, applauds the advances of modern industrialism. He views scientific mechanization as no threat to man, but rather as a means toward universal betterment, so long as the abuses of an uncontrolled industrialism are corrected. Norris, then, does not participate in the nature-machine conflict of earlier and later romantic writers. Rather, he substitutes for the machine the contemporary aesthetic movement, and—with some justice—views that movement as the major threat to the primitive values present in his conception of "life." He is thus caught up not so much in the realism-romanticism controversy of the nineties as in that decade's conflict between a decadent aestheticism and an emerging school of manliness, adventure, and the outdoors.

This second, more pertinent conflict is more clearly defined in England than in America, since our own aesthetic movement was primarily a weak imitation of English and French currents. In England, however, a genuine, vicious, and much publicized battle was fought between the school of Wilde, Beardsley, and the *Yellow Book* and that of Henley, Kipling, and Stevenson.[3] This struggle reached a climax in the trial of Wilde in 1895 and the apparent victory of the forces of "decency," virility, and moral art. But its ramifications continued into the early years of the new century, kept alive in part by the vogue of Bohemianism and by the discussion of Max Nordau's thesis in *Degeneration* that almost all modern art was degenerate.[4]

To Norris, therefore, as late as 1902 "literature" was characterized by the stylistics of Pater, by the "spirituality" of Ruskin, and most of all by Wilde's doctrine of the superiority of art to nature. "I was a man who stood in symbolic relations to the art and culture of my age," Wilde wrote in *De Profundis*, and one can see a rather twisted application of that statement in Norris's tendency to characterize "literature" in sexual terms as effeminate, with some suggestions of homosexuality. Indeed, much of the emotional force present in Norris's attack on literary style can only be understood in relation to his revulsion from the eroticism and homosexuality associated with Wilde, Beardsley and Huysmans.

In opposition to these figures was the group of writers, led by Henley, whom Jerome Buckley has called the "counter-decadents."[5] This counter movement reached its fulfillment in the work of Kipling. And just as Norris's description of "literature" often seems an epitome of the popular conception of Wilde, so his idea of "life" is intimately related both to the fiction and the aesthetic theory of Kipling. Like Norris, Kipling asserted the intrinsic value of both nature and machine. (The two faiths are strikingly combined in the two halves of *Captains Courageous*—the boy's "education" off the Grand Banks, the father's brilliant railroad journey.) Like Norris, Kipling posited aestheticism as the chief obstacle to the portrayal of "life," and like Norris he located aestheticism in literary centers and in universities. Almost all of Kipling's basic literary theory appears in *The Light That Failed*, which Norris read in the early 1890's. In that novel Dick, the artist-war correspondent, took part in battles and then painted them in all their violence, brutality, and dirt. He finds, however, that London art dealers and magazine editors want neat, tidy battle scenes, and he is almost led by them into painting pictures of that kind. Maisie, on the other hand, is a sheltered, imitative, innocuous painter concerned primarily with gaining public approval. This contrast, and Dick's frequently expressed contempt for "Art" (always capitalized), supplied Norris with much of the rhetoric of his "life"-"literature" antithesis.

It is not surprising, then, to find a Wilde-Kipling contrast running through Norris's descriptions of "literature" and "life," a contrast sharpened and vitalized by his personal rejection of the minor Bohemian worlds he encountered in San Francisco and New York.[6] Indeed, he tended in his later criticism to establish Kipling-like conflicts between the virile artist and a corrupting city aestheticism.[7] One of the best examples of this tendency, and also of Norris's basic "life"-"literature" antithesis, is his story "Dying Fires," published in 1902.[8] Although this is a work of fiction, it embodies a clear and forceful statement of Norris's critical ideas. It is therefore a more useful illustration of these ideas within the limitations of a brief paper than his rather diffuse essays.

"Dying Fires" tells of Overbeck, a young man born and raised in the Colfax mining district of the California Sierras. At the age of twenty-one, Overbeck writes a novel—*The Vision of Bunt McBride*—about the teamsters and waitresses, the dance halls and gambling joints of Colfax. It was a good novel, Norris stated, because

> young Overbeck had got started right at the very beginning. He had not been influenced by a fetich of his choice till his work was a mere replica of some other writer's. He was not literary. He had not much time for books. He lived in the midst of a strenuous, eager life, a

little primal yet; a life of passions that were often elemental in their simplicity and directness. [114]

This combination of elemental material and an unspoiled literary sensibility results in a powerful novel which brings Overbeck a call to New York. There he works in an editorial office and becomes a member of a literary set called "New Bohemia."

> It was made up of minor poets [Norris writes], whose opportunity in life was the blank space on a newspaper page below the end of an article; of men past their prime, who, because of an occasional story in a second-rate monthly, were considered to have "arrived"; of women who translated novels from the Italian and Hungarian; of decayed dramatists who could advance unimpeachable reasons for the non-production of their plays; of novelists whose books were declined by publishers because of professional jealousy on the part of the "readers." [119]

New Bohemia has its effect on Overbeck. Soon, Norris tells us,

> He could talk about "tendencies" and the "influence of reactions." Such and such a writer had a "sense of form," another a "feeling for word effects." He knew all about "tones" and "notes" and "philistinisms." He could tell the difference between an allegory and a simile. . . . An anticlimax was the one unforgivable sin under heaven. A mixed metaphor made him wince, and a split infinitive hurt him like a blow. [120]

The New Bohemians encourage him to write another novel, but one quite different from the "sane and healthy animalism" of *The Vision of Bunt McBride*. " 'Art must uplift,' " they tell him:

> Ah, the spiritual was the great thing. We were here to make the world brighter and better for having lived in it. The passions of a waitress in a railway eating-house—how sordid the subject. Dear boy, look for the

soul, strive to rise to higher planes! Tread upward; every book should leave a clean taste in the mouth, should tend to make one happier, should elevate, not debase. [122]

He begins a second novel, *Renunciations*, which Norris describes as a "city-bred story, with no fresher atmosphere than that of bought flowers. Its *dramatis personae* were all of the leisure class, opera-goers, intriguers, riders of blood horses." [123] (Norris seems to be using Henry James as a model here.) *Renunciations* is a failure, and Overbeck, realizing his mistake, returns to Colfax and attempts to rekindle his creative fires.

But the ashes were cold by now [Norris concludes]. The fire that the gods had allowed him to snatch . . . had been stamped out beneath the feet of minor and dilettante poets, and now the gods guarded close the brands that yet remained on the altars. [126–27]

"Dying Fires" is thus almost an allegory of Norris's beliefs about "life" and "literature," of his conviction that the best fiction derives from an untutored vision of the raw and violent in experience. But now one comes to a vital paradox in Norris's critical thought, one hinted at in "Dying Fires" when Norris noted of Overbeck's first novel that despite its power it revealed a "lack of knowledge of his tools" because of Overbeck's literary inexperience. For Norris combined with his primitivistic ideas an equally confirmed faith in what he called "the mechanics of fiction"—that is, a belief that the form and technique of fiction have certain rules, "tricks," and procedures which cannot only be described, but which can also be taught, and which must be acquired through arduous discipline and application. In other words, as far as the form of the novel is concerned, Norris attacked the instinctive, the emotional, the natural. He believed that fictional form is an intellectual problem in selection and organization for the achievement of plausibility, effect, and theme, and that there are few substitutes for a considered and painstaking intellectual solution. Commenting in 1901 on a proposed school of novel writing, Norris wrote:

Some certain people—foolish people—often say: "Teach people how to write novels! It must be born in you. There is no other way." I do not believe this. Nobody is born with the ability to write fiction. The greatest writers have to learn it all for themselves. If they taught themselves they could to a very large extent teach others. It is not at all impossible of belief that the fundamentals of construction in fiction could be in a manner codified, formalized and studied with as much good results as the fundamentals of any other of the professions.

All other of the fine arts demand preparatory courses of training—sculpture, painting, music, acting, architecture, and the like. Why should fiction be the one—the only one—to be ignored? Be well assured of this: The construction of a novel is as much of an exact science as the construction of a temple or a sonnet. The laws and rules of this construction have never been adequately formulated, but they exist.[9]

It is upon this fundamental duality, then, that Norris's critical system rests—"life, not literature" as far as theme and content are concerned, but "literature, not life" as far as form is concerned. Of the two, he gave the first priority. Without "life" as a foundation, no amount of technical training would benefit a writer. The best novelist, however, was he who was primitivistic in content and theme, sophisticated in form.

This duality in Norris's critical ideas anticipates and clarifies a major development in the American novel. There had always been a strong current of primitivistic anti-intellectualism in nineteenth-century American fiction, from Leatherstocking baiting the scientist Obed Bat in *The Prairie* to Huck Finn deciding to obey his heart rather than his conscience. This faith in the life of action, instinct, and emotion continues as a central force in the modern American novel, as in the work of Faulkner, Hemingway, and Steinbeck. There is little doubt that it is one of our distinctive national faiths.[10] The importance of Norris's criticism is not only that he is our earliest critic to found an aesthetic of the novel upon this faith, but also that he combines with his primitivism a demand that the novel be cultivated as an art form, and thereby represents a major bridge between the ungainly novels of a Cooper or Twain and the virtuoso techniques of a Hemingway or Faulkner. Much of our best modern fiction thus answers Norris's key demands, since it often combines an intense thematic primitivism with a striking facility in the manipulation of point of view, time, scene, and symbol. In short, the sophisticated primitivism which Norris required is a primary characteristic of twentieth-century American fiction. It is found both among our established novelists and among the more exciting postwar writers, such as Mailer, Bellow, and Styron. Whatever the crudities, the lapses, and the journalistic short-cuts of Norris's criticism, then, that criticism is important not only for the obvious reasons that it tells us much about Norris's own fictional practice and that it clarifies many of the literary issues of the time. His criticism is significant primarily because it increases our understanding of some of the most basic and seemingly most enduring characteristics of American fiction.

CRITICS OF HOWELLS'S *The Rise of Silas Lapham* have usually examined its subplot as an excrescence arising from a need to satisfy the popular demand for a romantic entanglement, as a digressive attack on the sentimental self-sacrifice of the "Tears, Idle Tears" variety, or as an overexpansion of the comedy of manners strain in the novel. Each of these points of view has a certain validity. But it is also true that the subplot and main plot have fundamentally similar themes, and that an examination of the thematic function of the subplot will elucidate both the ethical core of the novel and the relationship of that core to a prominent theme in Howells's later economic novels.[1]

ii

The main plot of *The Rise of Silas Lapham* concerns Silas's financial fall and moral rise. It revolves around his business affairs and social aspirations, and it concludes with his decision to sacrifice wealth and position rather than engage in business duplicity. The subplot centers on the triangle of Tom Corey and Irene and Penelope Lapham. Tom is mistakenly believed by all to be in love with Irene. The dilemma caused by his revelation that he loves Penelope is resolved when Irene is informed of the error. Irene then withdraws, leaving Tom and Penelope free to marry.

The dilemma or conflict within the subplot is solved by the use of an "economy of pain" formula.[2] Despite Penelope's willingness to sacrifice herself, Irene must be told of Corey's true sentiments, and Penelope and Corey must be encouraged to fulfill their love. In this way Irene suffers but Penelope and Tom are spared the pain of thwarted love. One rather than three suffers lasting pain. Of the three characters who determine the resolution of the subplot, Lapham realizes instinctively the correct course of action, Mrs. Lapham is helpless and hesitant—this despite her moralizing throughout the novel—and the clergyman Sewell articulates the principle involved and confirms Lapham's choice.

The problem which Silas must solve in the main plot parallels that in the subplot. The three groups who will be affected by his decision are he and his family (Lapham is a participant now as well as an arbiter), Rogers and his family, and the English agents who wish to purchase Lapham's depreciated mill.[3] The crucial point is that the Englishmen are more than mere scoundrels and more than the agents for an "association of rich and charitable people" [458]; they also represent society at large. This fact is somewhat obscured in the context of the financial trickery involved in the sale, since the agents are willing to be cheated. But Howells indicated the social implications of the sale when he immediately compared it to the defrauding of municipal governments. In both instances wealth and anonymity encourage dishonesty, and in both instances dishonesty undermines that which is necessary for the maintenance of the common good—effective city governments on the one hand, fair play and honest dealings in business affairs on the other. Lapham's refusal to sell therefore ultimately contributes to the well-being of society as a whole.

The thematic similarity in the two plots is that both involve a principle of morality which requires that the individual determine correct action by reference to the common good rather than to an individual need. Within the subplot this principle requires Lapham to choose on the basis of an "economy of pain" formula in which the fewest suffer. Within the main plot it requires him to weigh his own and Rogers's personal needs against the greater need of all men for decency and honesty. His "rise" is posited exactly in these terms, for at one point in the events leading up to his rejection of the Englishmen's offer he reflects quizzically that "It was certainly ridiculous for a man who had once so selfishly consulted his own interests to be stickling now about the rights of others." [466]

The method used to achieve moral insight is also similar in both plots. What is required is the ability to project oneself out of the immediate problem in which the personal, emotionally compelling need or desire is seen out of proportion to the need of the larger unit. In the subplot Mrs. Lapham finds this difficult, and Sewell asks her, " 'What do you think some one else ought to do in your place?' " [338] In the main plot it is no doubt Silas's realization of the honesty that he would ask of other men in a similar situation which aids him in making the same demand of himself. Lastly, as in the subplot, Silas is capable of moral insight, Mrs. Lapham again falters, and Sewell (at the end of the novel) attempts explanations.

One of the functions of the subplot is therefore to "double" the moral theme of the novel, to intensify and clarify it by introducing it within a narrower, more transparent dilemma. The subplot also plays other important roles. Dominating the center of the novel it is solved before the full exposition of Lapham's business crisis.[4] It occurs, in other words, between Howells's early remark that Lapham "could not rise" [67] to unselfishness in his dealings with Rogers and Lapham's own words at the close which indicate a concern for the "rights of others." The subplot thus contributes to the "education" of Lapham in the correct solution of moral problems. His moral rise is the product of more than a conscience troubled by his earlier treatment of Rogers. It is also the result of his ready absorption of the "economy of pain" formula as a moral guide in the subplot, a formula which he later translates into its exact corollary, the greatest happiness for the greatest number, when he is faced in the main plot with the more difficult problem of the ethical relationship of the individual to society. To sum up, the subplot of *The Rise of Silas Lapham* serves the functions of doubling the statement of the novel's theme, of foreshadowing the moral principle governing the main plot, and of introducing Lapham to the correct solution of moral problems.[5]

iii

It is possible, at this point, to suggest that the ethical core of the novel can be described as utilitarianism (as interpreted by John Stuart Mill), since both plots dramatize a moral principle in which the correct action is that which results in the greatest happiness for the greatest number. I do not wish to intimate that Howells consciously employed the ethical ideas of Mill. Rather, I believe that the similarity between Mill's utilitarianism and the ethical principles of *The Rise of Silas Lapham* is probably the result of parallel attempts to introduce the ethical teachings of Christ within social contexts and yet avoid supernatural sanctions. Howells's emerging Christian socialism in the late 1880's is well known,[6] and Mill wrote:

I must again repeat . . . that the happiness which forms the utilitarian standard of what is right in conduct, is not the agent's own happiness, but that of all concerned . . . . In the golden rule of Jesus of Nazareth, we read the complete spirit of the ethics of utility. To do as you would be done by, and to love your neighbour as yourself, constitute the ideal perfection of utilitarian morality.[7]

That Howells was conscious of the applicability of the Golden Rule to the theme of *The Rise of Silas Lapham* is clear, I believe, from his ironic use of it in connection with Rogers. When Rogers senses that Lapham may reject the Englishmen's offer, his appeal to Lapham is based on the premise that

In our dealings with each other we should be guided by the Golden Rule, as I was saying to Mrs. Lapham before you came in. I told her that if I knew myself, I should in your place consider the circumstances of a man in mine, who had honourably endeavoured to discharge his obligations to me, and had patiently borne my undeserved suspicions. I should consider that man's family, I told Mrs. Lapham. [462]

But Lapham's answer is the response of a man who is aware of the sophistry of a narrow use of the Golden Rule and who recognizes the necessity for the consideration of a wider range of obligation than individual need. " 'Did you tell her,' " he asks Rogers, " 'that if I went in with you and those fellows, I should be robbing the people who trusted them?' " [462]

iv

There is a twofold advantage in viewing the main and subplots of *The Rise of Silas Lapham* as controlled by a similar conception of moral behavior. First, the novel takes on a thematic unity and structural symmetry. It is within a single moral system, for example, that the apparent conflict between the attack on self-sacrifice in the subplot and Lapham's self-sacrifice in the main plot is reconciled. Penelope's self-sacrifice would diminish the sum total of happiness of those affected by her action, and therefore is wrong; Silas's self-sacrifice increases the happiness of mankind collectively, and therefore is right.[8] Secondly, the theme of the novel anticipates Howells's acceptance of Tolstoy's ethical ideals within the next few years and helps explain his response to those ideals once he encountered them. For in the two plots of *The Rise of Silas Lapham* Howells had already begun working out a belief that man must rise above himself and view life, as, he later explained, Tolstoy had taught him to view life, "not as a chase of a forever impossible personal happiness, but as a field for endeavor toward the happiness of the whole human family." [9] The conviction that man's primary commitment is to mankind was to be one of the themes which Howells emphasized in the series of novels from *Annie Kilburn* (1888) to *A Traveler from Altruria* (1894). In *The Rise of Silas Lapham* that theme appears in a less obvious social context (Howells had to strain for the connection between the English agents and society) and—more importantly—as an obligation which the average individual can grasp and fulfill. His novels during the years following the Haymarket crisis were to examine the theme of man's duty to his fellow men more intensively but less hopefully.

11   THE GARLAND-CRANE
RELATIONSHIP

HAMLIN GARLAND's reports of his meetings with Stephen Crane during 1891–94 have been heavily relied upon by Crane scholars in their accounts of these crucial years of Crane's career. Yet unlike Crane's equally important relationship with William Dean Howells,[1] there has been great difficulty in establishing the correct chronology of events in the association. Garland's autobiographical productivity is in part the cause of this difficulty, for, besides containing obvious lapses of memory within individual accounts, his reports also differ among themselves in significant details. He wrote four major descriptions of his relationship with Crane. The first, in the *Saturday Evening Post* of July, 1900, was occasioned by Crane's death the previous month. The second, in the April, 1914, *Yale Review*, was ostensibly prompted by Garland's chance reading of a paragraph on Crane a few months earlier. It was probably also the product of Garland's plumbing his memory for *A Son of the Middle Border*, which had begun appearing serially in *Collier's* and which contained a few paragraphs on Crane. The third account, in the *Bookman* for January, 1930, was a revision of the *Yale Review* article for the serialization of Garland's literary autobiography *Roadside Meetings*. His final report was a revision of the *Bookman* article for *Roadside Meetings* (1930).[2]

Crane's critics and biographers have been troubled by Garland's accounts. During the 1920's Thomas Beer politely quarreled with Garland in his biography of Crane,[3] and Wilson Follett failed to publish Garland's introduction to one of the volumes in Crane's collected works because of Garland's inaccuracies.[4] More recently John Berryman and R. W. Stallman have labored over Garland's recollections, with Stallman, in particular, attempting to unravel Garland's clearly tangled accounts.[5] One of the reasons readers of Garland's reports have been led astray is that they have known a great deal about Crane but not enough about Garland. The purpose of this essay is to describe the Garland-Crane relationship from the vantage point of a more detailed knowledge of Garland's activities of 1891–94 than has hitherto been brought to bear upon this subject.[6]

ii

According to Garland, he first met Crane in the summer of 1891 at Avon-by-the-Sea, a New Jersey resort, where Crane was aiding his brother to report shore news for the *New York Tribune* and where Garland was lecturing at the Seaside Assembly. Garland recalled that Crane had reported one of his lectures there and that Crane had told Garland about his article on the Junior Order of United American Mechanics' parade, which had caused Crane's dismissal from the *Tribune*. Garland's next remembered series of meetings with Crane was in New York eighteen months later. According to Garland, Crane sent him a copy of *Maggie* sometime during the winter of 1892–93 and then called upon him a number of times, including visits when he brought with him the manuscripts of *The Red Badge of Courage* and his earliest poems.

The major error that Garland made in his recollec-

tions was to telescope several of his meetings with
Crane. In reality, he met Crane at Avon-by-the-Sea in
August of both 1891 and 1892 and in New York in the
late winter and early spring of both 1893 and 1894.
The problem confronting a reader of Garland's accounts, therefore, is to determine whether an event
which Garland recollected as occurring in 1891 or 1893
happened in those years or in the years immediately
following.

The incidents that Garland placed in the summer of
1891 can be readily dated. In the spring of 1891, while
still teaching in Boston, Garland contracted to present
a series of "Lecture Studies in American Literature and
Expressive Art" at the Seaside Assembly from August
11 to August 25. His arrangements with Mr. and Mrs.
Alberti, the promoters of the Chautauqua-like assembly, also provided for incidental lectures on the single
tax and on miscellaneous literary subjects.[7] It was on
August 17 that he met Crane, for on the eighteenth
Crane reported Garland's lecture on Howells for the
Tribune, an occurrence from which Garland dated
their acquaintance.[8] The two young men met several
times during the remaining week of Garland's engage-
ment. Garland, a "published" writer (*Main-Travelled
Roads* had appeared in June), sufficiently impressed
Crane for the latter to inquire of Helen Trent on
September 10 if she had heard him lecture at Avon and
to describe his appearance as that of "a nice Jesus
Christ." [9]

Garland returned to the Seaside Assembly in late
August, 1892, and found Crane again reporting shore
news.[10] He had barely settled himself, however, when
on August 21 Crane's famous "On the New Jersey
Coast" article describing the Mechanics' parade was
published. Crane showed it to Garland about a week
afterward and told of being "let out" of his *Tribune*
job. That fall Crane moved to New York.

iii

The central fact in the Garland-Crane relationship of 1893 and 1894 is that most of the events
occurred in 1894, though Garland dated all of them
1893. In the fall of 1892 Garland undertook a two-
month tour of the West Coast, returning to Boston
(where he was still living) shortly after the new year.[11]
For the next three months (January–March, 1893),
though still considering Boston his home, he spent
much time in New York. On January 22, for example,
he and Howells visited Henry George in New York;[12]
yet on January 27 he was back in Boston to preside at a
meeting of the American Psychical Society.[13] He was
certainly in Boston in the latter half of February to
help out James A. Herne, who had just produced *Shore
Acres* at the Boston Museum.[14] It was, therefore, probably in early March, 1893, during one of his frequent
visits to New York, that Garland met the Albertis, who
had kept in touch with Crane and who informed him
that Crane was living in New York.[15] Shortly thereafter
Garland received in the mail a copy of *Maggie*; and it
was, no doubt, his recent meeting with the Albertis as
well as his recollection of Crane's style that led him to
identify Johnston Smith as Crane and to write asking
him to call.

The only other major incident in the relationship
that can definitely be assigned to 1893 is Garland's
bringing together of Crane and Howells. He advised
Crane to send a copy of *Maggie* to Howells and then
spoke to Howells about the novel when they met for
lunch on March 22.[16] Howells, however, did not get
around to reading the novel until a few days after
March 29, in response to a letter from Crane.[17] Between March 29 and April 8 Howells read *Maggie* and
he and Crane met.[18] Meanwhile, Garland had returned
to Boston, and in late March he left for a long tour of

the South and Far West. After completing his tour, he spent the summer and early fall in Chicago and West Salem, Wisconsin, not returning to the East until late October.[19]

It is difficult, then, to accept Stallman's theory that Crane brought the initial draft of *The Red Badge of Courage* and the earliest drafts of his poems to Garland in early 1893.[20] Beer, Berryman, and Stallman accept Crane's letter of April 2, 1893, to Mrs. Armstrong (in which he announced that he had just finished a war story) as the "birth notice" of *The Red Badge*.[21] On April 2 Garland was somewhere in the South, not to return to New York for over six months.[22] As for the poems, it is almost universally agreed that they were written after Crane heard Howells read from Emily Dickinson, and Crane had not yet met Howells on March 29.

Crane brought Garland *The Red Badge* and his poems in early 1894 rather than in early 1893. In all his accounts Garland stated that Crane visited him in New York at the apartment on One Hundred and Fifth Street in Harlem, which he was sharing with his brother Franklin. Garland also recalled that Franklin, an actor, was playing in Herne's *Shore Acres* at Daly's Theatre. *Shore Acres* began its New York run (after a successful spring season in Boston) on October 30, 1893, and transferred to Daly's Theatre on Christmas Day, where it ran until late May, 1894.[23] Garland had come to New York from the West for its opening in October,[24] but returned afterwards to Boston for almost two months in order to conduct a series of over thirty sittings with an exceptional psychic he had discovered in Los Angeles the previous year.[25] He came down to New York the third week in December,[26] and it was at that time that he established residence with his brother at 107 West One Hundred and Fifth

Street.[27] As far as the confusion in Garland's accounts is concerned, it appears that since his major and more extended meetings with Crane occurred at the One Hundred and Fifth Street apartment, he placed the 1893 *Maggie* meeting there as well. But since one of the few dates he could later check with accuracy was his June, 1893, review of *Maggie* in the *Arena*,[28] he was led to move the entire series of 1894 meetings back to 1893.

Garland lived with his brother in their Harlem apartment and revised the essays of *Crumbling Idols* until February 6 or 7, when he left for a lecture tour of the South and Midwest, returning to New York on March 10.[29] It was some time before this journey that Crane brought Garland his poems and startled him by composing one on the spot. He wrote it so effortlessly and smoothly that it seemed to Garland, who had just returned from almost six weeks of testing a psychic "for voices and the movement of objects without contact," [30] that Crane was the agent for a "ghost" writer. February is probably the best date for this event, since Corwin Linson recalled that Crane appeared with his newly written poems in mid-February, 1894,[31] and by mid-March Howells was writing Crane that magazine editors were not interested in the poems.[32] In April a number of them were read at the "Uncut Leaves" affair.[33] In short, Crane's " 'I wrote the things in February of 1893' " [34] is doubtless a typical Crane slip for "February of 1894."

Garland returned to New York from his western trip in early March. Apparently not hearing from Crane for some time, he wrote him on April 17 asking him to call.[35] Crane replied facetiously on April 18 [36] but did call within a few days, for on April 22 Garland wrote Crane that if he would "come to the stage door tomorrow night and ask for my brother he will hand

you the $15 and also a pass for 'Margaret Fleming'.
Don't trouble yourself about the borrowing," he continued. "We all have to do that sometimes." [37] The
borrowed $15 undoubtedly refers to the famous inci-
dent (narrated by Garland) of Crane lacking the
money to pay for the typing of *The Red Badge*, though
the typist had permitted him to claim half of the typed
manuscript. She would relinquish the other half on
payment of the fee of $15. It was with the first half
that Crane visited Garland between April 18 and 22.
Crane was having the manuscript typed at that time in
order to submit it either to *McClure's Magazine* or
to the McClure newspaper syndicate, for on May 8
Garland wrote Crane from Chicago asking if "Mc-
Clures finally [took] that war story for serial rights?" [38]
On November 15 Crane reported to Garland that
"McClure was a beast about the war-novel. . . . He
kept it for six months until I was near mad." [39]

Garland had left for Chicago on April 25, 1894,[40] in
order to take up permanent residence in that city and
in West Salem, where he had settled his parents. He
did not return to the East until December, 1895. His
few brief encounters with Crane in 1896 and 1898 are
of little interest or importance. In all, the relationship
was fruitful for both writers. Crane received encour-
agement and aid during a vital period of his career; [41]
Garland received the gratification of an important
discovery and a large store of personal recollections of
Crane, which he was later able to exploit. These
recollections are both invaluable and hazardous,
though it is hoped that the journey through them will
now be less difficult.

STEPHEN CRANE's *Maggie: A Girl of the Streets* has
often served as an example of naturalistic fiction in
America. Crane's novel about a young girl's fall and
death in the New York slums has many of the distinctive elements of naturalistic fiction, particularly a slum
setting and the theme of the overpowering effect of
environment. Crane himself appeared to supply a naturalistic gloss to the novel when he wrote to friends
that *Maggie* was about the effect of environment on
human lives. Yet the novel has characteristics which
clash with its neat categorization as naturalistic fiction.
For one thing, Crane's intense verbal irony is seldom
found in naturalistic fiction; for another, Maggie herself, though she becomes a prostitute, is strangely
untouched by her physical environment. She functions
as an almost expressionistic symbol of inner purity
uncorrupted by external foulness. There is nothing, of
course, to prevent a naturalist from depending on
irony and expressionistic symbolism, just as there is
nothing to prevent him from introducing a deterministic theme into a Jamesian setting. But in practice the
naturalist is usually direct. He is concerned with revealing the blunt edge of the powerful forces which condition our lives, and his fictional technique is usually
correspondingly blunt and massive. When Zola in

L'Assommoir and *Nana* wished to show the fall into prostitution of a child of the slums, his theme emerged clearly and ponderously from his full description of the inner as well as outer corruption of Nana and from his "realistic" symbolism. Crane's method, on the other hand, is that of obliqueness and indirection. Irony and expressionistic symbolism ask the reader to look beyond literal meaning, to seek beyond the immediately discernible for the underlying reality. Both are striking techniques which by their compelling tone and their distortion of the expected attempt to shock us into recognition that a conventional belief or an obvious "truth" may be false and harmful. Perhaps, then, *Maggie* can best be discussed by assuming from the first that Crane's fictional techniques imply that the theme of the novel is somewhat more complex than the truism that young girls in the slums are more apt to go bad than young girls elsewhere.[1]

The opening sentence of *Maggie* is: "A very little boy stood upon a heap of gravel for the honor of Rum Alley."[2] The sentence introduces both Crane's theme and his ironic technique. By juxtaposing the value of honor and the reality of a very little boy, a heap of gravel, and Rum Alley, Crane suggests that the idea of honor is inappropriate to the reality, that it serves to disguise from the participants in the fight that they are engaged in a vicious and petty scuffle. Crane's irony emerges out of the difference between a value which one imposes on experience and the nature of experience itself. His ironic method is to project into the scene the values of its participants in order to underline the difference between their values and reality. So the scene has a basic chivalric cast. The very little boy is a knight fighting on his citadel of gravel for the honor of his chivalrous pledge to Rum Alley. Crane's opening sentence sets the theme for *Maggie* because the novel is essentially about man's use of conventional but inapplicable abstract values (such as justice, honor, duty, love, and respectability) as weapons or disguises. The novel is not so much about the slums as a physical reality as about what people believe in the slums and how their beliefs are both false to their experience and yet function as operative forces in their lives.

Let me explore this idea by examining first the lives of the novel's principal characters and then the moral values which control their thinking about their lives. Crane uses two basic images to depict the Bowery. It is a battlefield and it is a prison. These images appear clearly in the novel's first three chapters, which describe an evening and night in the life of the Johnson family during Maggie's childhood. The life of the family is that of fierce battle with those around them and among themselves. The novel opens with Jimmie fighting the children of Devil's Row. He then fights one of his own gang. His father separates them with a blow. Maggie mistreats the babe Tommie; Jimmie strikes Maggie; Mrs. Johnson beats Jimmie for fighting. Mr. and Mrs. Johnson quarrel. Mrs. Johnson beats Maggie for breaking a plate; Mr. Johnson strikes Jimmie with an empty beer pail. Mr. Johnson comes home drunk and he and Mrs. Johnson fight—all this in three rather short chapters. Crane's fundamental point in these chapters is that the home is not a sanctuary from the struggle and turmoil of the world but is rather where warfare is even more intense and where the animal qualities encouraged by a life of battle—strength, fear, and cunning—predominate. The slum and the home are not only battlefields, however, but are also enclosed arenas. Maggie's tenement is in a "dark region," and her apartment, "up dark stairways and along cold, gloomy halls," [6] is like a cave. Crane's description of the Johnson children eating combines both the warfare and cave images into one central metaphor of primitive competition for food:

> The babe sat with his feet dangling high from a precarious infant's chair and gorged his small stomach. Jimmie forced, with feverish rapidity, the grease-enveloped pieces between his wounded lips. Maggie, with side glances of fear of interruption, ate like a small pursued tigress. [8]

By means of this double pattern of imagery, Crane suggests that the Johnsons' world is one of fear, fury, and darkness, that it is a world in which no moral laws are applicable, since the Johnsons' fundamental guide to conduct is an instinctive amorality, a need to feed and to protect themselves.

Once introduced, this image of the Bowery as an amoral, animal world is maintained throughout *Maggie*. Mr. Johnson dies, Jimmie assumes his position, and the Johnsons' family warfare continues as before. Maggie and Jimmie go to work, and each finds that struggle and enclosure mark his adult world. Jimmie becomes a belligerent truck driver, imprisoned by his ignorance and his distrust. He respects only strength in the form of the red fire engine which has the power to crush his wagon. Maggie works in a prisonlike sweat shop where she is chided into resentment by her grasping employer. Theirs are lives of animal struggle and of spiritual bleakness in which they only faintly realize their own deprivation. Maggie sits with the other girls in her factory workroom in a vague state of "yellow discontent," and Jimmie, the brawling teamster, "nevertheless . . . , on a certain star-lit evening, said wonderingly and quite reverently, 'Deh moon looks like hell, don't it?'" [17]

The moral values held by the Johnsons are drawn

almost entirely from a middle-class ethic which stresses
the home as the center of virtue, and respectability as
the primary moral goal. It is a value system oriented
toward approval by others, toward an audience. In the
opening chapter of the novel, Jimmie hits Maggie as
Mr. Johnson is taking them home. Mr. Johnson cries,
" 'Leave yer sister alone *on the street.*' " [6] (my
italics) The Johnsons' moral vision is dominated by
moral roles which they believe are expected of them.
These roles bring social approbation, and they are also
satisfying because the playing of them before an audience encourages a gratifying emotionalism or self-
justification. The reaction to Maggie's fall is basically
of this nature. She is cast out by her mother and
brother for desecrating the Home, and her seducer,
Pete, rejects her plea for aid because she threatens the
respectability of the rough and tumble bar in which he
works. The moral poses adopted by the Johnsons and
by Pete have no relation to reality, however, since the
home and the bar are parallel settings of warfare rather
than of virtue.

The key to the morality of the Bowery is therefore
its self-deceiving theatricality. Those expressing moral
sentiments do so as though playing a role before a real
or implied audience. Crane makes the dramatic nature
of Bowery morality explicit in scenes set in dance halls
and theatres. In a dance hall, an audience of Maggies,
Jimmies, and Petes listens enraptured to a song "whose
lines told of a mother's love, and a sweetheart who
waited, and a young man who was lost at sea under
harrowing circumstances." [26] Later, Maggie and
Pete see plays

> in which the dazzling heroine was rescued from the
> palatial home of her treacherous guardian by the hero
> with the beautiful sentiments. . . . Maggie lost herself
> in sympathy with the wanderers swooning in snow-
> storms beneath happy-hued church windows, while a

choir within sang "Joy to the World." To Maggie and
the rest of the audience this was transcendental realism.
Joy always within, and they, like the actor, inevitably
without. Viewing it, they hugged themselves in ecstatic
pity of their imagined or real condition. [29–30]

The audience identifies itself with maligned and innocent virtue despite the inapplicability of these roles to
their own lives. "Shady persons in the audience re-
volted from the pictured villainy of the drama. With
untiring zeal they hissed vice and applauded virtue.
Unmistakably bad men evinced an apparently sincere
admiration for virtue." [30]

This same ability to project oneself into a virtuous
role is present in most of the novel's characters. Each
crisis in the Johnson family is viewed by neighbors who
comprise an audience which encourages the Johnsons
to adopt moral poses. In the scene in which Maggie is
cast out, both Jimmie and Mrs. Johnson are aware of
their need to play the roles of outraged virtue in
response to the expectations of their audience. Mrs.
Johnson addresses the neighbors "like a glib showman," and with a "dramatic finger" points out to them
her errant daughter. [56] The novel's final scene is a
parody of Bowery melodrama. Mrs. Johnson mourns
over the dead Maggie's baby shoes while the neighbors
cry in sympathy and the "woman in black" urges her to
forgive Maggie. In the midst of her exhortations, "The
woman in black raised her face and paused. The
inevitable sunlight came streaming in at the window."
[68] Crane in this scene connects the sentimental
morality of melodrama and the sanctimoniousness of
Bowery religion. Both the theatre and the mission
purvey moral attitudes which have no relation to life
but which rather satisfy emotional needs or social
approval. The heroes and heroines of melodrama cannot be confronted with reality, but the church is
occasionally challenged. When it is, as when the mis-

sion preacher is asked why he never says "we" instead of "you," or when Maggie seeks aid from the stout clergyman, its reaction is either nonidentification with reality (" 'What?' " asks the preacher) or withdrawal from it (the clergyman sidesteps Maggie). It is as though the church, too, were a sentimental theatre which encouraged moral poses but which ignored the essential nature of itself and its audience.

Both of these central characteristics of the Bowery—its core of animality and its shell of moral poses—come together strikingly in Mrs. Johnson. There is a bitter Swiftian irony in Crane's portrait of her. Her drunken rages symbolize the animal fury of a slum home, and her quickness to judge, condemn, and cast out Maggie symbolizes the self-righteousness of Bowery morality. In a sense she symbolizes the entire Bowery world, both its primitive amorality and its sentimental morality. It is appropriate, then, that it is she who literally drives Maggie into prostitution and eventual death. Secure in her moral role, she refuses to allow Maggie to return home after her seduction by Pete, driving her into remaining with Pete and then into prostitution. Maggie is thus destroyed not so much by the physical reality of slum life as by a middle-class morality imposed on the slums by the missions and the melodrama, a morality which allows its users both to judge and to divorce themselves from responsibility from those they judge.

Crane's characterization of Maggie can now be examined. His description of her as having "blossomed in a mud-puddle" with "none of the dirt of Rum Alley . . . in her veins" [17] is not "realistic," since it is difficult to accept that the slums would have no effect on her character. Zola's portrait of Nana dying of a disfiguring disease which symbolizes her spiritual as well as physical corruption is more convincing. Crane's desire, however, was to stress that the vicious determin-

istic force in the slums was its morality, not its poor
housing or inadequate diet, and it is this emphasis
which controls his characterization of Maggie. His
point is that Maggie comes through the mud-puddle of
her physical environment untouched. It is only when
her environment becomes a moral force that she is
destroyed. Maggie as an expressionistic symbol of purity in a mud-puddle is Crane's means of enforcing his
large irony that purity is destroyed not by concrete
evils but by the very moral codes established to safe-
guard it.

But Maggie is a more complex figure than the above
analysis suggests. For though her world does not affect
her moral nature, it does contribute to her downfall by
blurring her vision. Her primary drive in life is to
escape her mud-puddle prison, and she is drawn to
Pete because his strength and elegance offer a means of
overcoming the brutality and ugliness of her home and
work. Her mistaken conception of Pete results from
her enclosed world, a world which has given her romantic illusions just as it has supplied others with
moral poses. Her mistake warrants compassion, however, rather than damnation and destruction. She is
never really immoral. Throughout her fall, from her
seduction by Pete to her plunge into the East River,
Crane never dispels the impression that her purity and
innocence remain. Her weakness is compounded out
of the facts that her amoral environment has failed to
arm her with moral strength (she "would have been
more firmly good had she better known how" [49]),
while at the same time it has blinded her with self-
destructive romantic illusions ("she wondered if the
culture and refinement she had seen imitated . . . by
the heroine on the stage, could be acquired by a girl
who lived in a tenement house and worked in a shirt
factory" [31]).

There is considerable irony that in choosing Pete

Maggie flees into the same world she wished to escape. Like Mrs. Johnson, Pete desires to maintain the respectability of his "home," the bar in which he works. Like her, he theatrically purifies himself of guilt and responsibility for Maggie's fall as he drunkenly sobs " 'I'm good f'ler, girls' " [63] to an audience of prostitutes. And like Maggie herself, he is eventually a victim of sexual warfare. He is used and discarded by the "woman of brilliance and audacity" just as he had used and discarded Maggie. In short, Maggie can escape the immediate prison of her home and factory, but she cannot escape being enclosed by the combination of amoral warfare (now sexual) and moral poses which is the pervasive force in her world.

In his famous inscription to *Maggie*, Crane wrote that the novel "tries to show that environment is a tremendous thing in the world and frequently shapes lives regardless." But he went on to write that "if one proves that theory one makes room in Heaven for all sorts of souls (notably an occasional street girl) who are not confidently expected to be there by many excellent people." [3] The second part of the inscription contains an attack on the "many excellent people" who, like Maggie's mother, immediately equate a fallen girl with evil and hell. Crane is here not so much expressing a belief in heaven as using the idea of salvation and damnation as a rhetorical device to attack smug, self-righteous moralism. The entire novel bears this critical intent. Crane's focus in *Maggie* is less on the inherent evil of slum life than on the harm done by a false moral environment imposed on that life. His irony involving Mrs. Johnson, for example, centers on the religious and moral climate which has persuaded her to adopt the moral poses of outraged Motherhood and despoiled Home.

Maggie is thus a novel primarily about the falsity and destructiveness of certain moral codes. To be sure, these codes and their analogous romantic visions of experience are present in Maggie's environment, and are in part what Crane means when he wrote that environment shapes lives regardless. But Crane's ironic technique suggests that his primary goal was not to show the effects of environment but to distinguish between moral appearance and reality, to attack the sanctimonious self-deception and sentimental emotional gratification of moral poses. He was less concerned with dramatizing a deterministic philosophy than in assailing those who apply a middle class morality to victims of amoral, uncontrollable forces in man and society. *Maggie* is therefore very much like such early Dreiser novels as *Sister Carrie* and *Jennie Gerhardt,* though Dreiser depends less on verbal irony and more on an explicit documentation and discussion of the discrepancy between an event and man's moral evaluation of an event. *Maggie* is also like *The Red Badge of Courage,* for the later novel seeks to demonstrate the falsity of a moral or romantic vision of the amorality which is war.

Crane, then, is a naturalistic writer in the sense that he believes that environment molds lives. But he is much more than this, for his primary concern is not a dispassionate, pessimistic tracing of inevitable forces but a satiric assault on weaknesses in social morality. He seems to be saying that though we may not control our destinies, we can at least destroy those systems of value which uncritically assume we can. If we do this, a Maggie (or a Jennie Gerhardt) will at least be saved from condemnation and destruction by an unjust code.

Writers who seek greater justice, who demand that men evaluate their experience with greater clarity and honesty, are not men who despair at the nature of things. They are rather critical realists. Like William Dean Howells, Crane wishes us to understand the inadequacies of our lives so that we may improve them. Although Crane stresses weaknesses in our moral vision rather than particular social abuses, there is more continuity between Howells's critical realism and Crane's naturalism than one might suspect. This continuity is not that of subject matter or even of conception of man and society. It is rather that of a belief in the social function of the novel in delineating the evils of social life. If one sees such a writer as Crane in this light, the often crude and outdated determinism of early American naturalism lessens in importance. One begins to realize that American naturalism, like most vital literary movements, comprised a body of convention and assumption about the function and nature of literature which unprescriptively allowed the writer to use this shared belief as the basis for a personally expressive work of art. Crane's fiction is therefore permanently absorbing and historically significant not because he was a determinist or fatalist writing about the slums or about the chaos of war. His fiction still excites because his ironic technique successfully involves us in the difference between moral appearance and reality in society. His fiction is historically important because his expression of this theme within the conventions of naturalistic fiction reveals the relationship between critical realism and naturalism. But his fiction is perhaps even more significant historically because he revealed the possibility of a uniquely personal style and vision within naturalistic conventions. Our writers have responded to the critical spirit and the fictional sensationalism and freedom of naturalism without a sense of being burdened by doctrinaire precepts and forms. And it is no doubt this invigorating freedom within continuity which has been one of the principal reasons for the strength and influence of the naturalistic movement in America, from Crane and Dreiser to our own times.

13 SYNTHETIC CRITICISM AND FRANK NORRIS'S *THE OCTOPUS*

ONE OF THE MOST significant recent movements in the interpretation of American literature has been the revitalization of the critical method of V. L. Parrington. Like Parrington, such writers as Marius Bewley, Richard Chase, Leslie Fiedler, and Leo Marx synthesize "main currents" in American literature and thought. Again like Parrington, they posit initially a universal dialectic in American experience which accounts for the distinctively American quality of these patterns in our culture. In many ways this movement has been estimable. It has illumined large areas of our national experience and expression. It has also proved that a brilliant critic can forge intellectual history and myth criticism into an exciting and revealing tool of cultural research.

Yet despite my admiration for much synthetic criticism, I am troubled by certain misgivings and reservations concerning its usefulness as a tool of literary criticism, and would like to explain these doubts. My example of a work of synthetic criticism is Leo Marx's "Two Kingdoms of Force," [1] an article which I will examine in relation to Frank Norris's *The Octopus*. I choose Mr. Marx as an example of a synthetic critic because I find him the most satisfying and the most suggestive of the group I have named, and am therefore moved to examine his critical method as representative of the group. I choose *The Octopus* as my example of a literary work not because I wish to explicate it (I have published explications elsewhere), and not because Mr. Marx's comments on it are more or less satisfying than those on other works. Rather, I know more about Norris's novel than any other work discussed by Mr. Marx, and can best demonstrate my general thesis by using it. In addition, I will introduce W. F. Taylor's *The Economic Novel in America* to help clarify the issues involved in my discussion.

Mr. Marx believes that a "common denominator" in much American literature is "the opposition between two cardinal images of value. One usually is an image of landscape, either wild or, if cultivated, rural; the other is an image of industrial technology." This opposition is not the result of a writer's direct reference to the historical fact of industrialism. Rather, the impact of industrialism has caused opposing "psychic states" to cluster around the opposing images of the landscape and the machine. These states are above all those suggesting love on the one hand and power on the other—that is, accommodation to the organic creativity of nature or dominion over nature. Though at first certain romantic writers (Hawthorne, Thoreau) consciously symbolized this opposition by means of images of nature and the machine , within a short time the dramatic clash between nature and machine became crystallized into a literary convention whose use suggests a writer's subconscious acceptance of the conflict rather than his explicit reference to it. Whether conscious or not, however, the polarity between the kingdom of love and the kingdom of power—almost always represented by images of nature and technology—is to Mr. Marx "a dominant, probably *the* dominant theme in our literature."

In a key passage, Mr. Marx explains that in *Huckle-berry Finn* the destruction of the raft by the steamboat reveals Twain's participation in this theme despite Twain's avowed faith in industrial progress and despite his lack of conscious symbolism in the incident. "In the face of a discrepancy," Mr. Marx writes, "between what a writer tells us directly, in his own words, so to speak, and what is implied by his work, it is to his work that we owe the more serious attention. As between mere opinion and the indirection of art, we assume that art springs from the more profound and inclusive experience."

Almost all the literary works and passages cited by Mr. Marx to support his view are highly persuasive, including the scene in *The Octopus* in which Presley experiences the massacre of a flock of sheep by a railroad engine. This incident, Mr. Marx points out, destroys the idyllic calm of the scene as well as Presley's sense of oneness with nature. Norris's presentation of the railroad and nature thus appears little different from that of a Hawthorne or Thoreau. Mr. Marx concludes: "Presley listens to the agonized cries of the wounded animals and the blood seeping down into the cinders, *and thus the theme of the novel is set.*" [2]

In his discussion of *The Octopus*, Mr. Marx has followed a procedure common in synthetic criticism: the critic derives a broad pattern from particular images, passages, and scenes in a large number of works by many authors; he then implies that this pattern is the key to the themes of individual works. The opportunities for error and misdirection in this method are familiar to readers of doctoral dissertations which survey extensive material. In such works the student establishes a tradition, "places" particular authors in this tradition, and finally deduces an interpre-

tation and evaluation of individual works in terms of
the author's tradition. On a more sophisticated level
the same danger is inherent in recent works of synthetic criticism.

Let me begin to explain more concretely the source
of my doubts about synthetic criticism by comparing
Mr. Marx's interpretation of late nineteenth-century
American fiction with that of W. F. Taylor, who has
written one of the standard works on the subject. Mr.
Taylor studies the economic fiction (in a broad sense)
of most of the major figures of the age—Howells,
Twain, Norris, and Garland—and of many minor writers as well. He believes that the novelists of this
period

> put on record—indeed, with virtual unanimity they put
> on *favorable* record—the coming of the Machine. Sel-
> dom if ever do they make the Machine *per se* the object
> of critical attack . . . . In America, in the course of the
> conquest of the immense distances, the immense re-
> sources of a continent, the usefulness of the Machine
> was a thing difficult indeed to call in question; and,
> whether because of a tacit understanding of that
> difficulty, or because of some other causative factor,
> American novelists practically never did so. Instead,
> they mostly agreed with Mark Twain in welcoming the
> Machine, seeing in mechanical power, properly con-
> trolled, simply a means of realizing the old democratic
> dream of universal material well-being.
>
> What our novelists put on *un*favorable record, what
> they subjected to telling exposure and criticism, was not
> the Machine itself but the misuse of the Machine by
> Society; not industrialism *per se*, but the workings of an
> industrial order administered by a *laissez-faire* capital-
> ism.[3]

Mr. Taylor thus states a "pattern" antithetical to
Mr. Marx's. If one reads *The Octopus* in terms of Mr.
Taylor, its theme is the misuse of the machine by an

uncontrolled monopoly rather than distrust and fear of the machine itself. But perhaps the antithesis between Mr. Marx and Mr. Taylor demonstrates not that one is right and the other wrong, but that *The Octopus* is a complex novel which is many things to many critics. Perhaps, too, this antithesis can be resolved by a reading of the novel which tries to come to grips with its own intrinsic pattern.[4]

Norris borrowed from Joseph Le Conte, one of his teachers at the University of California, the idea that God is immanent in nature as a universal force or energy, and he used this idea as the core theme of *The Octopus*. As Presley views the harvested wheat fields toward the end of the novel, he "seemed for one instant to touch the explanation of existence." The explanation is that "FORCE only existed—FORCE that brought men into the world, FORCE that crowded them out of it to make way for the succeeding generation, FORCE that made the wheat grow, FORCE that garnered it from the soil to give place to the succeeding crop." This universal force inherent in the life processes of both human and nonhuman existence is finally characterized by Presley as "primordial energy flung out from the hand of the Lord God himself, immortal, calm, infinitely strong." [5] In *The Octopus* this energy is symbolized primarily by the wheat and by the processes of its growth and the "laws" of its production and distribution. Although these processes and laws are impersonal, they benefit the race as a whole. Individuals or groups determine their personal destinies by recognizing these processes—that is, by recognizing God in nature—and by tuning their lives in accord with them.

The moral center of the novel is thus nature, and evil is the failure to understand the processes of nature or the attempt to thwart them. Within this thematic core, the novel has a twofold structure. First, three overly intellectual and fundamentally selfish young men—Annixter, Vanamee, and Presley—come to accept the benevolence and the omnipotence of the natural cycle of birth, death, and rebirth. By this action, they rise above their personal sorrows and narrowness, and thereby achieve contentment and a resolution of their problem. Second, the ranchers and the railroad fail to realize the omnipotence and benevolence of the natural law of supply and demand which determines the production and the distribution of wheat. Both groups greedily exploit the demand for wheat, the first by speculative "bonanza" farming, the second by monopoly of transportation. Norris hammers at this similarity early in Book II in parallel images of the ranchers and railroad "sucking dry" the land. First, he describes a railroad map of California, on which the railroad's lines are drawn in red:

> The map was white, and it seemed as if all the colour which should have gone to vivify the various counties, towns, and cities marked upon it had been absorbed by that huge, sprawling organism, with its ruddy arteries converging to a central point. It was as though the State had been sucked white and colourless, and against this pallid background the red arteries of the monster stood out, swollen with life-blood, reaching out to infinity, gorged to bursting; an excrescence, a gigantic parasite fattening upon the life-blood of an entire commonwealth. [II, 5]

The greed of the railroad is matched by that of the ranchers, however, for

> they had no love for their land. They were not attached to the soil. They worked their ranches as a quarter of a century before they had worked their mines. To husband the resources of their marvellous San Joaquin, they considered niggardly, petty, Hebraic. To get all there

was out of the land, to squeeze it dry, to exhaust it, seemed their policy. When, at last, the land worn out, would refuse to yield, they would invest their money in something else; by then, they would all have made fortunes. They did not care. "After us the deluge." [II, 14]

Both groups, moreover, engaged in corrupt acts in their struggle for possession of the profitable land and its crop. There is no doubt, of course, that Norris considered the railroad trust the more culpable of the two, and that he indirectly suggested means of alleviating its hold upon the community. But Norris's primary emphasis was that the benevolent cycle of growth and the fulfilment of demand by supply are completed regardless of whatever harm and destruction men bring down upon themselves by their attempts to hinder or to manipulate these natural processes for their own profit.[6]

The symbolic role of the railroad engine throughout *The Octopus* is conditioned by the theme of the novel. Individual engines, such as that which destroys the flock of sheep, do not symbolize the machine as a power antithetical to that of nature. Rather, they symbolize a particular railroad company whose monopolistic practices are antithetical to a particular natural law. Norris underlines this symbolism at the close of the passage which ends the description of the sheep massacre:

Then, faint and prolonged, across the levels of the ranch, he heard the engine whistling for Bonneville. Again and again, at rapid intervals in its flying course, it whistled for road crossings, for sharp curves, for trestles; ominous notes, hoarse, bellowing, ringing with the accents of menace and defiance; and abruptly Presley saw again, in his imagination, the galloping monster, the terror of steel and steam, with its single eye, Cyclopean, red, shooting from horizon to horizon; but saw it now as the symbol of a vast power, huge, terrible, flinging the echo of its thunder over all the reaches of the valley, leaving blood and destruction in its path; the leviathan, with tentacles of steel clutching into the soil, the soulless Force, the iron-hearted Power, the monster, the Colossus, the Octopus. [I, 48]

The engine, then, is above all a symbol of the Octopus—that is, the Trust. The monopoly is the soulless Force whose practices, spreading death and destruction, are opposed to the landscape ("tentacles of steel clutching into the soil"). Norris desires to engage our emotions to fear and hate trusts, not industrialism or the machine. His theme in the novel is not the conflict between technology and nature or between the kingdom of power and the kingdom of love, as Mr. Marx suggests it is in his discussion of the sheep massacre scene. His theme is that "all things, surely, inevitably, resistlessly work together for good," [II, 361] that technology and the landscape are allied rather than opposed in the forward thrust toward human betterment. They are allied, that is, so long as men use both landscape and machine (the means of production and distribution of wheat) in accordance with natural law.

Norris illustrates this possible alliance by means of Cedarquist, a San Francisco industrialist and shipbuilder. Early in Book II Cedarquist outlines to Magnus Derrick a plan whereby the producers and distributors of wheat can use the law of supply and demand in a way which benefits both themselves and mankind. He explains:

The great word of this nineteenth century has been Production. The great word of the twentieth century will be . . . Markets. As a market for our Production—or let me take a concrete example—as a market for our

Wheat, Europe is played out. Population in Europe is not increasing fast enough to keep up with the rapidity of our production. In some cases, as in France, the population is stationary. *We*, however, have gone on producing wheat at a tremendous rate. The result is over-production. We supply more than Europe can eat, and down go the prices. The remedy is *not* in the curtailing of our wheat areas, but in this, we *must have new markets, greater markets*. For years we have been sending our wheat from East to West, from California to Europe. But the time will come when we must send it from West to East. . . . I mean, we must look to China. Rice in China is losing its nutritive quality. The Asiatics, though, must be fed; if not on rice, then on wheat. . . . What fatuous neglect of opportunity to continue to deluge Europe with our surplus food when the East trembles upon the verge of starvation! [II, 21–22]

On the basis of this perception, Cedarquist begins to ship wheat to the East. In short, the "mechanical" distributor (a railroad or shipping company) can with profit to himself aid the fulfilment of a benevolent natural law rather than attempt to thwart the operation of the law for excessive personal gain.

Norris therefore does establish a kingdom of love, but he not unconventionally suggests that it is the kingdom of self-love, of greed—not of power—which opposes it. In other words, Norris's basic attitude corresponds less to the artist's sense that there is a contradiction between the worlds of nature and the machine than to the capacity of the popular mind to maintain without a sense of contradiction the opposing ideals of cultural primitivism and industrial progress. Norris holds in solution, without conflict, both the kingdom of love (accommodation to nature) and of power (dominion over nature), just as most eighteenth-century Englishmen (as Lois Whitney has pointed out) [7] called for both a return to the simple and a progress toward the complex, and just as the average American feels no discrepancy in taking a jet to "get away from it all" in the North Woods.

Now in this cursory summary of *The Octopus* I have not taken up what Mr. Marx considers "direct" testimony as evidence concerning Norris's attitude toward the machine. I have not, for example, discussed his California background, in which the importance of the railroad to the well-being of the state was universally affirmed but in which the Southern Pacific monopoly was often referred to as an Octopus. I have not traced those occasions in Norris's fiction and criticism when he deals honorifically with the industrialist and with machines, including railroad engines. I have not introduced the influence of Kipling, who combined in such works as *Captains Courageous* an admiration both for the "natural" life and for railroads and their machinery. Nor have I discussed Zola's influence on Norris's depiction of destructive railroad engines and on his practice of animalizing machines. I have not taken up any of these, though they have all helped me to understand Norris's treatment of the railroad in *The Octopus*.

But to return to one of Mr. Marx's most pertinent ideas (which he introduces in connection with Huck's raft and the steamboat), that though a fictional incident may not be literally symbolic of a nature-machine conflict, it may draw upon the conventional imagery and connotations of such a conflict. This observation is applicable to *The Octopus*. Though Norris does not distrust the machine, he does mistrust monopolies. He therefore uses the conventional imagery of the machine-nature "pattern" to add emotional intensity to his engine-Octopus-Trust symbolism. In short, the machine-nature antithesis serves Norris as a reservoir of affective imagery, though it does not necessarily function as a thematic key.

Norris's exploitation of the machine as a source of such imagery is also demonstrated by a passage in which nature itself is presented as a destructive machine. In this passage, Norris wished to depict how the omnipotent and impersonal power of nature appears to a timid, withdrawn, and frightened person, one whose timidity prevents her from sensing the fundamental benevolence of this power. To Mrs. Derrick, therefore, the railroad and nature are equally destructive because of their power. She first imagines the railroad (repeating Presley's imagery) as a "galloping terror of steam and steel, with its single eye, Cyclopean, red" etc. [I, 173] Then follows her conception of nature:

> She recognized the colossal indifference of nature, not hostile, even kindly and friendly, so long as the human ant-swarm was submissive, working with it, hurrying along at its side in the mysterious march of the centuries. Let, however, the insect rebel, strive to make head against the power of this nature, and at once it became relentless, a gigantic engine, a vast power, huge, terrible; a leviathan with a heart of steel, knowing no compunction, no forgiveness, no tolerance, crushing out the human atom with soundless calm, the agony of destruction sending never a jar, never the faintest tremor through all that prodigious mechanism of wheels and cogs. [I, 174]

Thus, it is apparent that Norris draws upon machine imagery to provide emotional intensity to the description of any destructive force, including nature itself when it is so conceived. This reliance does indeed imply that despite his overt emphasis on the benevolent role of the machine, Norris unconsciously participates in the "main current" described by Mr. Marx.

But I do not think that it is possible on the basis of this participation to say that *The Octopus* is "really about" the two kingdoms of force—that is, that its theme is set by its imagery of the destructive machine.

Rather, I think it more meaningful to say that Mr. Taylor has seen that Norris's theme involves an attack on the misuse of the machine, and that Mr. Marx has seen that Norris relies on a traditional romantic description of the machine. Both have described parts of Norris's theme and art in *The Octopus;* neither has seen the novel whole; and neither, indeed, have I in this brief paper.

How, then, to strive for this "wholeness"? I would suggest a critical eclecticism. To know something of Norris's biography, of the intellectual and literary influences upon him, and of his social milieu—to read *The Octopus* with a sense of its total impact and with a recognition that its parts (including imagery and symbolism) should be relevant to that impact—*and* to know something about such cultural traditions as the "two kingdoms of force"—this seems to me to be the best method for determining the meaning and significance of a complex work of art. The conflict between the two kingdoms of force may well be the dominant theme in American literature, and Norris does partake of that theme in *The Octopus.* But the theme of *The Octopus* is not "set" by scenes in which one element is the conventional imagery of the destructive machine.

NOTES

1 — Late Nineteenth-Century American Realism

1. "Realism: An Essay in Definition," X (June, 1949), 184–97; expanded and revised into "Modern Realism as a Literary Movement," *Documents of Modern Literary Realism*, ed. George J. Becker (Princeton, 1963), pp. 3–38. Other recent attempts to define realism (besides the standard literary glossaries, handbooks, and dictionaries) are: Harry Levin, "What is Realism?" *Comparative Literature*, III (Summer, 1951), 193–98; Everett Carter, "The Meaning of, and in, Realism," *Antioch Review*, XIII (Spring, 1952), 78–94; and René Wellek, "The Concept of Realism in Literary Scholarship," *Concepts of Criticism* (New Haven, 1963), pp. 222–55. Erich Auerbach, *Mimesis: The Representation of Reality in Western Literature* (Princeton, 1953), and Lionel Trilling, "Reality in America," *The Liberal Imagination* (New York, 1950), pp. 3–21, are stimulating discussions of what writers have considered to be reality, but neither undertakes a full definition of realism as a literary mode. Bernard R. Bowron, Jr., "Realism in America," *Comparative Literature*, III (Summer, 1951), 200–17, skirts a definition.

2. Although Becker actually divides realism into three categories (the realistic mode, realism of subject matter, and philosophical realism), I have confined my discussion to the first. He notes of the second category that it is "no more than an outgrowth and extension of the first, but it is so important that we should disengage it and look at it separately, calling it realism of subject matter." He defines the third category as "pessimistic determinism" or naturalism, "a philosophical position taken by some realists." I discuss this third category in my essay on naturalism.

2 – Late Nineteenth-Century American Naturalism

1. Richard Chase, *The American Novel and Its Tradition* (Garden City, N. Y., 1957), p. 186 *n*; George J. Becker, "Modern Realism as a Literary Movement," in *Documents of Modern Literary Realism*, ed. George J. Becker (Princeton, 1963), p. 35. See also the definitions by Lars Ahnebrink, *The Beginnings of Naturalism in American Fiction* (Cambridge, Mass., 1950), pp. vi–vii; Malcolm Cowley, "A Natural History of American Naturalism," *Documents*, pp. 429–30; and Philip Rahv, "Notes on the Decline of Naturalism," *Documents*, pp. 583–84.

2. The discussion of naturalism in the next two paragraphs resembles in several ways that by Charles C. Walcutt in his *American Literary Naturalism, A Divided Stream* (Minneapolis, 1956), pp. 3–29. In general, I accept Walcutt's analysis of naturalism's philosophical and literary ambivalences. I believe, however, that his discussion of the naturalists' divided view of nature and of their maintenance of the idea of free will by implicitly encouraging their readers to social action are ways of describing these ambivalences historically and socially – by source and effect – rather than as they function within the naturalistic novel itself.

3. Erich Auerbach's *Mimesis: The Representation of Reality in Western Literature* (Princeton, 1953) deals with the representation of these ideas in imaginative literature from antiquity to our own day.

4. Frank Norris, "A Plea for Romantic Fiction," *The Literary Criticism of Frank Norris*, ed. Donald Pizer (Austin, Texas, 1964), p. 77.

5. *The Complete Edition of Frank Norris* (Garden City, N. Y., 1928), VIII, 269. References to this edition of *McTeague* will hereafter appear in the text.

6. I discuss this aspect of Norris's thought at some length in my "Evolutionary Ethical Dualism in Frank Norris' *Vandover and the Brute* and *McTeague*," PMLA, LXXVI (December, 1961), 522–60.

7. Lionel Trilling, "Reality in America," *The Liberal Imagination* (New York, 1950).

8. Theodore Dreiser, *Sister Carrie* (Modern Library Edition), p. 554.

9. See particularly William A. Freedman, "A Look at Dreiser as Artist: The Motif of Circularity in *Sister Carrie*," *Modern Fiction Studies*, VIII (Winter, 1962–63), 384–92.

10. Stephen Crane, *The Red Badge of Courage and Selected Prose and Poetry*, ed. William M. Gibson (New York, 1956), p. 275. References to this edition will appear hereafter in the text.

3 — Frank Norris's Definition of Naturalism

1. "A Plea for Romantic Fiction," *Boston Evening Transcript*, December 19, 1901, p. 14; "Zola as a Romantic Writer," *Wave*, XV (June 27, 1896), 3; "Frank Norris' Weekly Letter," *Chicago American Literary Review*, August 3, 1901, p. 5. The first essay was republished in *The Responsibilities of the Novelist* (New York, 1903); the second was partially reprinted in Franklin Walker, *Frank Norris: A Biography* (Garden City, N. Y., 1932). The third essay was republished, along with the first two, in *The Literary Criticism of Frank Norris*, ed. Donald Pizer (Austin, Texas, 1964). Quotations refer to *The Literary Criticism of Frank Norris*.

2. "Zola as a Romantic Writer," p. 71.

3. "A Plea for Romantic Fiction," p. 76.

4. *Ibid.*   5. *Ibid.*, p. 78.

6. "Zola as a Romantic Writer," p. 72.

7. It was not uncommon throughout Zola's career for critics to call him a romanticist because of his sensational plots, though such critics usually intended disparagement rather than praise. See Max Nordau, *Degeneration* (New York, 1895), pp. 494–97, and F. W. J. Hemmings, *Émile Zola* (Oxford, 1953), p. 74.

8. "Frank Norris' Weekly Letter," p. 75.

9. This choice of novels is not entirely clear, but perhaps it can be explained by the contemporary reputation of the three works and by the fact Norris was writing for a newspaper supplement. *La Débâcle* was well received in America, while *La Terre* was attacked for its gross sex-

uality and *Fécondité* was heavily criticized for its excessive polemicism.

10. "Frank Norris' Weekly Letter," p. 75.

11. "Zola as a Romantic Writer," p. 72.

12. See Zola's *The Experimental Novel and Other Essays* (New York, 1893), pp. 17–18, and Lars Åhnebrink, *The Beginnings of Naturalism in American Fiction* (Cambridge, Mass., 1950), pp. vi–vii; and Charles C. Walcutt, *American Literary Naturalism, A Divided Stream* (Minneapolis, 1956), pp. vii–viii.

13. Norris to Marcosson, November, 1899, in *The Letters of Frank Norris*, ed. Franklin Walker (San Francisco, 1956), p. 48.

4—The Evolutionary Foundation of W. D. Howells's Criticism and Fiction

1. See Herbert Edwards, "Howells and the Controversy over Realism in American Fiction," *American Literature*, III (November, 1931), 237–48, and Leonard Lutwack, "William Dean Howells and the 'Editor's Study,'" *ibid.*, XXIV (May, 1952), 195–207.

2. *Howells and the Age of Realism* (Philadelphia, 1954), p. 190. See also Robert P. Falk, "The Literary Criticism of the Genteel Decades: 1870–1900," *The Development of American Literary Criticism*, ed. Floyd Stovall (Chapel Hill, 1955), p. 137.

3. *Howells and the Age of Realism*, p. 190.

4. Three surveys of evolutionary criticism are: Harry H. Clark, "The Influence of Science on American Literary Criticism, 1860–1910 . . . ," *Transactions of the Wisconsin Academy of Sciences, Arts and Letters*, XLIV (1955), 109–64; René Wellek, "The Concept of Evolution in Literary History," *Concepts of Criticism* (New Haven, 1963), pp. 37–53; and Thomas Munro, "Evolutionary Theories of Literature," *Evolution in the Arts* (New York, 1963), pp. 145–52.

5. For a descriptive analysis of this work, see Donald Pizer, *Hamlin Garland's Early Work and Career* (Berkeley and Los Angeles, 1960), pp. 13–21.

6. *Ibid.*, pp. 17–18.   7. *Ibid.*, pp. 18–19.

8. Herbert Spencer, *First Principles* (New York, 1885 [1862]), p. 517. Faith in progress was, of course, a traditional American belief, but in the late nineteenth century it found renewed support in the evolutionary philosophy of Herbert Spencer. See Richard Hofstadter, *Social Darwinism in American Thought, 1860–1915* (Philadelphia, 1945), pp. 18–36.

9. (New York, 1886), p. [v]. Posnett was educated at Cambridge, was associated with Trinity College, Dublin, and from 1886 was Professor of Classics and English Literature at University College, Auckland, New Zealand. For a summary of his position and an account of its derivation, see his "The Science of Comparative Literature," *Contemporary Review*, LXXIX (1901), 855–72.

10. Hutcheson M. Posnett, *Comparative Literature* (New York, 1886), p. 20.

11. (New York, 1883), p. vi.

12. *Ibid.*, p. ix. The relationship between the genius (or great man) and evolutionary progress was much discussed in the eighties. See Philip P. Wiener, *Evolution and the Founders of Pragmatism* (Cambridge, Mass., 1949), pp. 129–36.

13. Thomas S. Perry, *English Literature in the Eighteenth Century* (New York, 1883), p. ix.

14. For Perry and Symonds, see Virginia Harlow, *Thomas Sergeant Perry: A Biography* (Durham, N. C., 1950), pp. 103–5, 119–21.

15. Perry, *A History of Greek Literature* (New York, 1890), p. 297. Although not published until 1890, this work was completed in 1885. See Harlow, *T. S. Perry*, p. 139.

16. See particularly Harry H. Clark, "The Role of Science in the Thought of W. D. Howells," *Transactions of the Wisconsin Academy of Sciences, Arts and Letters*, XLII (1953), 263–303; also Carter, *Howells and the Age of Realism*, pp. 91–102, and Edwin H. Cady, *The Road to Realism* (Syracuse, 1956), pp. 147–51.

17. For an account of the close literary and personal relationship between Howells and Perry, see Virginia Harlow, "William Dean Howells and Thomas Sergeant Perry,"

Boston Public Library Quarterly, I (October, 1949), 135–50. Howells wrote to Perry on March 3, 1886, that he had told a friend "that *I had learned from you* the new and true way of looking at literature." *Life in Letters of William Dean Howells*, ed. Mildred Howells (Garden City, N. Y., 1928), I, 379. Howells became aware of Garland's critical ideas when the two men met in the summer of 1887.

18. *Harper's New Monthly Magazine*, LXXIII (1886) 318.

19. *Ibid.*, LXXIV (December, 1886), 161–62 and LXXXII (April, 1891), 803–4.

20. *Criticism and Fiction* (New York, 1891), pp. 1–2. Citations hereafter appear in the text.

5 – Evolution and Criticism: Thomas Sergeant Perry

1. A 235-page essay published in *Gately's World's Progress. A General History of the Earth's Construction, and of the Advancement of Mankind in the Various Lines of Scientific and Industrial Action Which Have Led to the Present State of Civilization*, ed. Charles E. Beale (Boston, 1886).

2. This work was completed in late 1885.

3. See, for example, E. A. Robinson's comments in his *Selections from the Letters of Thomas Sergeant Perry* (New York, 1929), pp. 5, 9; and John T. Morse, Jr., *Thomas Sergeant Perry: A Memoir* (Boston, 1929), pp. 27, 45–46.

4. "All the past shows how simple the truth is," he wrote in early 1882 (Virginia Harlow, *Thomas Sergeant Perry: A Biography* [Durham, N. C., 1950], p. 18). See also Thomas S. Perry, "Science and the Imagination," *North American Review*, CXXXVII (July, 1883), 56, in which he remarked that "every great step in thought" is "a simplification of knowledge."

5. See "The Progress of Literature," *Gately's World's Progress*, p. 834, and Perry, "Science and the Imagination," p. 56.

6. Although Virginia Harlow devotes a chapter in her

biography to Perry's criticism of the eighties, her emphasis is primarily biographical and descriptive. I am indebted to her admirable work, however, for much of my knowledge of Perry's life and career.

7. Letter to Mrs. Perry, March, 1882; published by Harlow, pp. 117–18.

8. Perry, *English Literature in the Eighteenth Century* (New York, 1883), p. 398.

9. Letter to Moorfield Storey, 1882; published by Harlow, p. 118.

10. Perry, *John Fiske* (Boston, 1906), p. 32.

11. Perry read Spencer's *First Principles* while in college (Harlow, p. 19) and later reviewed his *Study of Sociology* in the *Atlantic Monthly*, XXXIII (February, 1874), 238. John Fiske was a disciple of Spencer, and Perry no doubt acquired some of his Spencerian leanings from Fiske. Examples of Perry's explicit use of Spencer's evolutionary formula can be found in "The Progress of Literature," p. 770, and *A History of Greek Literature* (New York, 1890), pp. 138, 300.

12. Perry, *From Opitz to Lessing: A Study of Pseudo-Classicism in Literature* (Boston, 1885), pp. 143–44. See also Perry's "Science and Conscience," *Popular Science Monthly*, XXIII (May, 1883), 14–15.

13. *A History of Greek Literature*, p. 20.

14. *From Opitz to Lessing*, p. 140.

15. *English Literature in the Eighteenth Century*, p. vi.

16. *Ibid.*

17. *Ibid.*, p. ix. See also *From Opitz to Lessing*, pp. 121–22.

18. *English Literature in the Eighteenth Century*, p. ix.

19. *Ibid.*, pp. ix–x.

20. *A History of Greek Literature*, p. 191.

21. *From Opitz to Lessing*, p. v.

22. For Perry and Symonds, see Harlow, pp. 103–5. In his Preface to *English Literature in the Eighteenth Century* Perry acknowledged a debt to the volumes on Italian literature in Symonds's *Renaissance in Italy*. Symonds

frequently discussed genres as species throughout the seventies and eighties, though he gave the idea its most explicit exposition in his essay "On the Application of Evolutionary Principles to Art and Literature," *Essays Speculative and Suggestive* (London, 1890).

23. *A History of Greek Literature*, pp. 10–11.

24. *Ibid.*, p. 297.

25. *Ibid.*, p. 306. See also *ibid.*, p. 217.

26. *Ibid.*, p. 306.

27. I have omitted discussing Perry's belief that the literary tastes and conventions of an age were an additional environmental conditioning factor. He used this idea primarily to explain what he believed to be the failure of great seventeenth- and eighteenth-century writers to achieve great works of art.

28. *From Opitz to Lessing*, p. 58.

29. See Sholom J. Kahn, *Science and Aesthetic Judgment: A Study in Taine's Critical Method* (New York, 1953).

30. *English Literature in the Eighteenth Century*, pp. vi–vii.

31. *A History of Greek Literature*, p. 502.

32. *English Literature in the Eighteenth Century*, p. 16.

33. "William Dean Howells," *Century*, XXIII (March, 1882), 682.

34. *A History of Greek Literature*, p. 719.

35. *Ibid.*, p. 12.   36. *Ibid.*, p. 503–4.

37. *Ibid.*, p. 874.   38. *Ibid.*

39. *English Literature in the Eighteenth Century*, p. 242.

40. *Ibid.*, p. 241.

41. *Ibid.*, pp. 21–22.   42. *Ibid.*, p. 37.

43. *From Opitz to Lessing*, p. 15, and *English Literature in the Eighteenth Century*, p. 21.

44. "The Progress of Literature," p. 773.

45. *From Opitz to Lessing*, p. 114.

46. "Science and the Imagination," p. 53.

47. "The Progress of Literature," p. 834. See also Perry's "Science and Conscience," p. 14.

48. "William Dean Howells," p. 683.

49. *Ibid.*, p. 685.

50. "The Progress of Literature," p. 788.

51. *The Evolution of the Snob* (Boston, 1887), p. 63.

52. "The Progress of Literature," p. 834.

53. *Ibid.*, p. 835.

54. *A History of Greek Literature*, p. 12.

55. See, for example, John Dewey, "The Philosophical Work of Herbert Spencer," *Philosophical Review*, XIII (March, 1904), 157–79.

6 – Evolutionary Criticism and the Defense of Howellsian Realism

1. See John Dewey, *The Influence of Darwin on Philosophy* (New York, 1910), pp. 1–19, and David F. Bowers, "Hegel, Darwin, and the American Tradition," *Foreign Influences in American Life*, ed. David F. Bowers (Princeton, 1944), pp. 146–71.

2. Adapted from John Addington Symonds's "On the Application of Evolutionary Principles to Art and Literature," *Essays Speculative and Suggestive* (London, 1890).

3. See Virginia Harlow, "William Dean Howells and Thomas Sergeant Perry," *Boston Public Library Quarterly*, I (October, 1949), 135–50.

4. Virginia Harlow, *Thomas Sergeant Perry: A Biography* (Durham, N. C., 1950), p. 100.

5. See "George Pellew," *Critic*, XX (February 27, 1892), 133–34, and W. D. Howells, "George Pellew," *Cosmopolitan*, XIII (September, 1892), 527–30. Pellow died in 1892 at the age of 32.

6. Howells to Henry James, December 25, 1886; published in *Life in Letters of William Dean Howells*, ed. Mildred Howells (Garden City, N. Y., 1928), I, 388. Pellew also knew John Fiske and dedicated an unpublished philosophical work to him. See Ethel F. Fisk, *The Letters of John Fiske* (New York, 1940), p. 532.

7. Hamlin Garland, *Roadside Meetings* (New York, 1930), pp. 29–30, 55–61. Garland's dating in *Roadside Meetings* is haphazard, however, and the above dates

have been derived from contemporary records of his activities. It is of interest to note that Garland, Perry, Pellew, and Howells exhibited a sense of reciprocal indebtedness during the 1880's. Perry dedicated his second critical work, *From Opitz to Lessing* (1884), to Howells (his first, *English Literature in the Eighteenth Century* [1883], had been dedicated to John Fiske). Howells, on his part, remarked in 1886 that he *"had learned from* [Perry] the new and true way of looking at literature" (Howells to Perry, March 3, 1886; *Life in Letters*, I, 379). Pellew dedicated his Harvard Bowdoin Prize essay on *Jane Austen's Novels* (1883) to Perry as "A Student of His 'English Literature in the Eighteenth Century,'" and Perry himself acknowledged Pellew's "valuable suggestions" in his Preface to the latter work. In 1891 Garland attributed a "tremendous early debt to Howells and a later one to the critic Perry" ("The Latest Western Novelist," *Boston Evening Transcript*, June 15, 1891, p. 6).

8. Garland's reviews, all laudatory, are "Lemuel Barker," *Boston Evening Transcript*, January 31, 1887, p. 6 (*The Minister's Charge*); "April Hopes," *Transcript*, March 1, 1888, p. 6; "Annie Kilburn," *Transcript*, December 27, 1888, p. 6; Mr. Howells's Latest Novel," *Transcript*, December 14, 1889, p. 10, and "A Great Book," *Standard*, February 5, 1890, pp. 5–6 (both of *A Hazard of New Fortunes*). For an account of a typical Garland lecture in support of Howells, see "Howells Discussed at Avon-by-the-Sea," *New York Tribune*, August 18, 1891, p. 5.

9. Pellew, *Boston Post*, February 27, 1888, p. 3.

10. Garland, "Literary Emancipation of the West," *Forum*, XVI (October, 1893), 161.

11. Donald Pizer, *Hamlin Garland's Early Work and Career* (Berkeley and Los Angeles, 1960), pp. 17–18.

12. Garland, *New England Magazine*, N.S. II (May, 1890), 248–49.

13. *Ibid.*, p. 250.

14. Harlow, *Thomas Sergeant Perry*, p. 117.

15. *Ibid.*, p. 118.

16. Perry, *A History of Greek Literature* (New York, 1890), p. 20.

17. Perry, *English Literature in the Eighteenth Century* (New York, 1883), p. ix.

18. Perry, *From Opitz to Lessing: A Study of Pseudo-Classicism in Literature* (Boston, 1885), p. 15.

19. Perry, *English Literature in the Eighteenth Century*, p. 16.

20. Perry, *A History of Greek Literature*, p. 12.

21. *Ibid.*, pp. 503–4.   22. *Ibid.*, p. 12.

23. Perry, "William Dean Howells," *Century*, XXIII (March, 1882), 683.

24. *Ibid.*, p. 635.

25. Pellew to Garland, February 4, 1888, in the University of Southern California Library. This library also contains Garland's copy of Pellew's *Jane Austen's Novels*, inscribed to him by Pellew on March 9, 1888. I wish to thank the University of Southern California Library for permission to use this material from its Hamlin Garland Collection.

26. Pellew, *Jane Austen's Novels* (Boston, 1883), p. [5].

27. *Ibid.*, p. 47.   28. *Ibid.*, p. 48.

29. Pellew, *Forum*, V (July, 1888), 570.

30. Pellew, *Critic*, XVIII (January 17, 1891), 29.

31. *Ibid.*, p. 31.

32. Howells to Perry, April 14, 1888; *Life in Letters*, I, 414. Pellew's Letter to the Editor was in reply to a *Post* editorial which had attacked Howells's praise of Zola in the March "Editor's Study."

33. Pellew, *Boston Post*, February 27, 1888, p. 3.

34. *Ibid.*

7—Evolutionary Ideas in Late Nineteenth-Century English and American Literary Criticism

1. See Morse Peckham, "Darwinism and Darwinisticism," *Victorian Studies*, III (September, 1959), 19–40, for an explanation of the relatively negligible influence of the theory of natural selection. In terms of Peckham's defi-

nitions, the evolutionary ideas which I discuss are for the most part "Darwinisticistic"—that is, they owe less to the theory of natural selection than to other ideas of emergence and development which were popularized or introduced as a result of the impact of Darwinism.

2. *Comparative Literature* (New York, 1886), p. 20. This volume was published in Appleton's International Scientific Series.

3. "The Philosophy of Evolution," *Essays Speculative and Suggestive* (London, 1907 [1890]), p. 5.

4. "On the Application of Evolutionary Principles to Art and Literature," *ibid.*, p. 28.

5. See Donald Pizer, *Hamlin Garland's Early Work and Career* (Berkeley and Los Angeles, 1960), pp. 13–21.

6. *Comparative Literature* (New York, 1886).

7. *From Opitz to Lessing: A Study of Pseudo-Classicism in Literature* (Boston, 1885), pp. 143–44. See also H. H. Boyesen, "The Evolution of the German Novel," *Essays on German Literature* (New York, 1892), p. 232, and Brander Matthews, *The Development of the Drama* (New York, 1903), p. 351.

8. "American Literary Criticism and the Doctrine of Evolution," *International Monthly*, II (August, 1900), 153.

9. "The Evolution of American Thought," quoted by Pizer, *Garland's Early Work*, pp. 17–18. See also George Pellew, "The New Battle of the Books," *Forum*, V (July, 1888), 570.

10. "American Literary Criticism and the Doctrine of Evolution," *International Monthly*, II (July, 1900), 41.

11. Symonds, "On the Application of Evolutionary Principles to Art and Literature," *Essays Speculative and Suggestive* (London, 1890), pp. 27–52; Perry, *A History of Greek Literature* (New York, 1890), p. 859; and "The Progress of Literature," *Gately's World's Progress*, ed. Charles E. Beale (Boston, 1886), p. 661.

12. *Criticism and Fiction* (New York, 1891), pp. 18–22, 119.

13. *Ibid.*, p. 24.

14. *A History of Greek Literature*, p. 297.

15. *From Opitz to Lessing*, p. 140.

16. *Criticism and Fiction*, p. 88.

17. See, for example, Payne, "American Literary Criticism," p. 40. The "spontaneous variation" conception of literary greatness was reinforced in the early twentieth century by De Vries's mutation theory.

18. *Crumbling Idols* (Chicago and Cambridge, Mass., 1894), p. 191.

19. "On the Application of Evolutionary Principles," p. 37.

20. "On Some Principles of Criticism," *Essays Speculative and Suggestive*, pp. 53–78.

21. *Criticism and Fiction*, p. 30.

22. *From Opitz to Lessing*, p. 58.

23. "The Scientific Movement and Literature," *Studies in Literature*, 1789–1877 (London, 1899 [1878]), p. 106.

24. "American Literary Criticism," p. 45.

25. *Ibid.*, p. 39.

26. *Comparative Literature*, p. 76.

27. "American Literary Criticism," p. 149.

28. These beliefs were, of course, encouraged by other movements in nineteenth-century thought besides the direct influence of evolutionary ideas on critics and scholars—notably cultural anthropology, sociology, and linguistics. But each of these was itself partially a product of the widespread diffusion of evolutionary ideas. In short, modern historical literary scholarship owes much to nineteenth-century evolutionary thought, and the direct impact of evolutionary ideas on late nineteenth-century critics is perhaps the most clearly discernible and emphatic example of this debt.

8—Hamlin Garland and Stephen Crane: The Naturalist as Romantic Individualist

1. *The American Mind* (Boston, 1912), pp. 3–46. Cf. Richard D. Mosier, *The American Temper* (Berkeley, 1952).

2. Garland, *Crumbling Idols* (Chicago and Cambridge, Mass., 1894), p. vii. Citations hereafter appear in the text.

3. See Philip P. Wiener, *Evolution and the Founders of Pragmatism* (Cambridge, Mass., 1949).

4. Eugène Véron, *Aesthetics*, trans. W. H. Armstrong (Philadelphia, 1879), p. [v]. This copy of Véron is in the Hamlin Garland Collection, University of Southern California Library. All unpublished material cited hereafter is in the University of Southern California Library. I wish to thank Mrs. Constance Garland Doyle for permission to quote from Garland's unpublished work, and the University of Southern California Library for permission to consult its Hamlin Garland Collection.

5. Véron, p. xv.

6. *Ibid.*, p. xxii. Sometime during October–November, 1886, Garland copied this passage into his March 3, 1886, notebook ("Literary Notes. Vol. I" on spine; "March 3/86" on flyleaf).

7. *Ibid.*, p. 369.

8. In Garland's March 3, 1886, notebook, shortly after a sketch dated March 20, 1887.

9. "Ibsen as a Dramatist," *Arena*, II (June, 1890), 77–78.

10. When originally published in "The Literary Emancipation of the West," *Forum*, XVI (October, 1893), this passage was directed specifically at Western authors. It began, "Stand up, O young man and woman of the West!" and it also called upon Western writers to "Reject the scholasticism of the East." In *Crumbling Idols*, however, the passage was taken out of context to serve in the "Recapitulatory After-Word" where Garland clearly wished to broaden the range of his plea.

11. *Stephen Crane: An Omnibus*, ed. R. W. Stallman (New York, 1952), p. xix.

12. See Marcus Cunliffe, "Stephen Crane and the American Background of *Maggie*," *American Quarterly*, VII (Spring, 1955), 31–44.

13. *Stephen Crane: Letters*, ed. R. W. Stallman and

Lillian Gilkes (New York, 1960), p. 14; hereafter referred to as *Letters*.

14. The program for the full schedule of lectures has been published by Lars Åhnebrink, *The Beginnings of Naturalism in American Fiction* (Cambridge, Mass., 1950), pp. 442–43.

15. "Howells Discussed at Avon-by-the-Sea," *New York Tribune*, August 18, 1891, p. 5. Republished by Donald Pizer, "Crane Reports Garland on Howells," *Modern Language Notes*, LXX (January, 1955), 37–39.

16. *Letters*, p. 62.

17. To Lily B. Munroe, March, 1894; *ibid.*, p. 31.

18. William Dean Howells, *Criticism and Fiction* (New York, 1891), p. 145.

19. Letter to Miss Catherine Harris, November 12, 1896; *Letters*, p. 133.

20. Letter to John N. Hilliard January, 1896; *ibid.*, p. 110.

9—The Significance of Frank Norris's Literary Criticism

1. Franklin D. Walker, *Frank Norris: A Biography* (Garden City, N.Y., 1932), pp. 1–5.

2. It should be clear that I use "primitivistic" in its cultural rather than chronological sense. Norris's primitivism establishes certain key values in nature; he does not claim that these values flourished more in the past than in the present.

3. See Jerome Buckley, *The Victorian Temper* (Cambridge, Mass., 1951) and William Gaunt, *The Aesthetic Adventure* (New York, 1945).

4. See Grant C. Knight, *The Critical Period in American Literature* (Chapel Hill, 1951), pp. 70–75.

5. Jerome Buckley, *William Ernest Henley: A Study in the "Counter-Decadence" of the 'Nineties* (Princeton, 1945).

6. See James D. Hart's Introduction to Gelett Burgess, *Bayside Bohemia: Fin de Siècle San Francisco and Its Little Magazines* (San Francisco, 1954).

7. See "Frank Norris' Weekly Letter," *Chicago American,* August 24, 1901 and "New York as a Literary Center," syndicated January 19, 1902. The two articles are reprinted in *The Literary Criticism of Frank Norris,* ed. Donald Pizer (Austin, Texas, 1964), pp. 30–33, 36–40.

8. *Smart Set,* VII (July, 1902), 95–101. Citations in the text refer to the republication of the story in *The Complete Edition of Frank Norris* (Garden City, N. Y., 1928), IV, 113–27.

9. "Frank Norris' Weekly Letter," *Chicago American,* June 8, 1901: reprinted in *The Literary Criticism of Frank Norris,* pp. 9–10.

10. For discussions of the literary expression of this faith, see Philip Rahv, "The Cult of Experience in American Writing," *Image and Idea* (New York, 1949) and Lionel Trilling, "Reality in America," *The Liberal Imagination* (New York, 1950).

10 – The Ethical Unity of *The Rise of Silas Lapham*

1. The most satisfying explications of the novel are by George Arms, *The Rise of Silas Lapham,* Rinehart Editions (New York, 1949), pp. v–xvi; Everett Carter, *Howells and the Age of Realism* (Philadelphia, 1954), pp. 164–69; Edwin H. Cady, *The Road to Realism* (Syracuse, 1956), pp. 230–40; and George N. Bennett, *William Dean Howells: The Development of a Novelist* (Norman, Okla., 1959), pp. 150–61. Cady and Carter have also written excellent introductions to reprints of the novel in the Riverside Editions and Harper's Modern Classics series, respectively. Carter comes closest to discussing the theme of the novel as I do, though he defines it differently and does not analyze the relationship between the main plot and the subplot. See also John E. Hart, "The Commonplace as Heroic in *The Rise of Silas Lapham,*" *Modern Fiction Studies,* VIII (Winter, 1962–63), 375–83.

2. *The Rise of Silas Lapham* (Boston, 1885), p. 338. Citations hereafter appear in the text.

3. Although Howells hints that the agents are counter-

feit rather than real Englishmen, I have followed him in designating them as English.

4. By the close of Chapter xix Irene has been told of Tom's preference, Lapham has given Tom permission to continue courting Penelope, and Penelope has indicated (in the final words of Chapter xix) that it will only be a matter of time before she will accept Tom. The problem of the depreciated mill is introduced in the next chapter.

5. Mrs. Lapham's ethical values are a foil to those which Lapham ultimately practices. Her moral beliefs are strongly held but are fragmented; she is helpless and uncertain when a conflict of interests is present and a universal moral criterion is needed.

6. See particularly Clara M. Kirk, *W. D. Howells, Traveler from Altruria, 1889–1894* (New Brunswick, N. J., 1962).

7. *Utilitarianism, Liberty, and Representative Government*, Everyman's Library, p. 16.

8. Cf. Mill, *Utilitarianism*, pp. 15–16. "The utilitarian morality does recognize in human beings the power of sacrificing their greatest good for the good of others. It only refuses to admit that the sacrifice is itself a good. A sacrifice which does not increase, or tend to increase, the sum of happiness, it considers as wasted. The only self-renunciation which it applauds, is devotion to the happiness, or to some of the means of happiness, of others; either of mankind collectively, or of individuals within the limits imposed by the collective interests of mankind."

9. Howells, *My Literary Passions* (New York, 1895), p. 251.

11 – The Garland-Crane Relationship

1. For Howells and Crane, see Thomas A. Gullason, "New Light on the Crane-Howells Relationship," *New England Quarterly*, XXX (September, 1957), 389–92; and Edwin H. Cady, *The Realist at War* (Syracuse, 1958), pp. 212–18.

2. Hamlin Garland, "Stephen Crane: A Soldier of Fortune," *Saturday Evening Post*, CLXXIII (July 28,

1900), 16–17; "Stephen Crane as I Knew Him," *Yale Review*, N.S., III (April, 1914), 494–506; "Roadside Meetings of a Literary Nomad," *Bookman*, LXX (January, 1930), 523–28; *Roadside Meetings* (New York, 1930), pp. 189–206, et passim. The *Saturday Evening Post* article was reprinted in the *Book-Lover*, II (September–November, 1900), 6–9. The major differences (besides numerous minor variations) among the four accounts are: the *Post* dates the Avon meeting as 1888 or 1889, Garland's receiving *Maggie* in New York as 1891, and *The Red Badge* and poetry incidents as the autumn of 1892. It is the only account that indicates a considerable lapse of time between the *Maggie* and *Red Badge* incidents. The *Yale Review* has Crane bringing Garland first *The Red Badge* and then his poetry, whereas the *Post* and *Roadside Meetings* reverse this order. The *Bookman* has Crane showing *Maggie* to Garland at Avon in 1891 and omits all mention of the poetry manuscripts. See also the brief section on Crane in *A Son of the Middle Border* (New York, 1917), pp. 441–42.

3. Thomas Beer, *Stephen Crane: A Study in American Letters* (New York, 1923), pp. 246–47.

4. Follett asked Garland to write an introduction to Vol. III of Crane's collected works but returned the introduction with a letter requesting a revision of Garland's chronology (letters, Follett to Garland, November 15 and December 4, 1924, in the University of Southern California Library). Garland apparently failed to comply with the request, for Vol. III appeared with an introduction by Follett himself. I wish to thank the University of Southern California Library, the New York State Library, the Yale University Library, and the Columbia University Library for making available to me unpublished material referred to in this essay.

5. John Berryman, *Stephen Crane* (New York, 1950), and *Stephen Crane: An Omnibus*, ed. R. W. Stallman (New York, 1952). See particularly Stallman's attack (pp. 212–17, 565–67) on Berryman's version of the relationship.

6. Since the initial publication of this essay two additional critics have dealt with the Garland-Crane relationship: Olov W. Fryckstedt, "Crane's *Black Riders*: A Discussion of Dates," *Studia Neophilologica*, XXXIV (1962), 282–93, and Robert Mane, "Une Rencontre Littéraire: Hamlin Garland et Stephen Crane," *Études Anglais*, XVII (January–March, 1964), 30–46.

7. Letters, Garland to William Alberti, January 23, 30, and April 14, 1891, in the New York State Library, Albany, N. Y.

8. "Howells Discussed at Avon-by-the-Sea," *New York Tribune*, August 18, 1891, p. 5. Republished by Donald Pizer, "Crane Reports Garland on Howells," *Modern Language Notes*, LXX (January, 1955), 37–39. Garland recalled that Crane reported him on "The Local Novelists" (the lecture immediately after that on Howells), but since no report of such a lecture appears in the *Tribune*, and since there is a report of Garland's Howells lecture, it is clear that the Howells lecture is the one that Crane reported and that Garland recalled commending for its accuracy the next day.

9. Beer, p. 60.

10. The *New York Tribune*, August 15, 1892, p. 4, reported that Garland would arrive at Avon the following week. Victor Elconin has surveyed Crane's 1892 shore reporting in "Stephen Crane at Asbury Park," *American Literature*, XX (November, 1948), 275–89.

11. *A Son of the Middle Border*, pp. 445–58, and Garland's journal "Los Angeles, Fresno, Portland, Pasadena," in the University of Southern California Library.

12. *Life in Letters of William Dean Howells*, ed. Mildred Howells (Garden City, N. Y., 1928), II, 31.

13. *Psychical Review*, I (February, 1893), 290.

14. Garland, "On the Road with James A. Herne," *Century*, LXXXVIII (August, 1914), 579.

15. He received Crane's address from Mrs. Alberti, he recalled in *Roadside Meetings*. It was probably the Albertis who had informed Crane of Garland's presence in New York and who had supplied Crane with his address.

16. Howells wrote to Garland on March 19, 1893, asking him to come for lunch on the 22nd (letter in the University of Southern California Library). Crane wrote to Howells on March 28, inquiring whether Howells had read *Maggie* as yet and adding: "Mr. Garland has, I believe, spoken to you of it." In *Stephen Crane: Letters*, ed. R. W. Stallman and Lillian Gilkes (New York, 1960), p. 16; hereafter referred to as *Letters*. Howells recalled the circumstances of his first meeting with Crane in a letter to Cora Crane, July 29, 1900. *Ibid.*, p. 306. It was also probably during March, 1893, that Garland introduced Crane's work to B. O. Flower, editor of the *Arena*, whom Garland knew well. See Crane's letter to Lily Brandon Munroe, April, 1893, *ibid.*, p. 21.

17. In his letter to Crane, March 29, 1893, Howells explained that he had not as yet had a chance to read *Maggie. Ibid.*, p. 17.

18. In his letter to Crane, April 8, 1893, Howells praised *Maggie* and spoke of their "pleasant interview." *Ibid.*, p. 18.

19. Garland's journals (in the University of Southern California Library) "In the South. Washington, New Orleans, Memphis" and "Colorado and the West (Summer, '93)."

20. See *Stephen Crane: An Omnibus*, pp. 212–14, 565, and *Letters*, pp. 37, 50, 95.

21. Beer, p. 98; Berryman, p. 66; *Letters*, p. 17.

22. His journal "In the South" has him in Chattanooga on April 1 and in Atlanta on April 3.

23. George C. D. Odell, *Annals of the New York Stage*, XV (New York, 1949), 556–57.

24. Garland, "On the Road with James A. Herne," p. 579.

25. The sittings ran from November 3 to December 10, 1893. See Hamlin Garland, T. E. Allen, and B. O. Flower, "Report of Dark Seances, with a Non-Professional Psychic, for Voices and the Movement of Objects without Contact," *Psychical Review*, II (November, 1893 – February, 1894), 152–77.

26. He was still in Boston on December 16 but was in New York on December 19 (letters, Garland to Herbert S. Stone, December 16, 19, 1893, in the Yale University Library).

27. This address appears in Garland's correspondence for the first time in his letter to Herbert S. Stone, December 19, 1893 (in the Yale University Library). It continues to appear in his letters as his New York address until late April, 1894, when he left the city. Garland and Crane renewed their friendship very soon after Garland settled in New York in late December, for by January 2 Garland was using Crane as a messenger to return a manuscript to S. S. McClure (see *Letters*, p. 29).

28. "An Ambitious French Novel and a Modest American Story," *Arena*, VIII (June, 1893), xi–xii.

29. Letter, Garland to E. C. Stedman, February 5, 1894, in the Columbia University Library, and Garland's journal "Notes by the Way," in the University of Southern California Library.

30. See the title of Garland's article in the *Psychical Review* (n. 25 above).

31. Corwin K. Linson, *My Stephen Crane*, ed. Edwin H. Cady (Syracuse, 1958), pp. 48–49.

32. Howells to Crane, March 18, 1894, *Letters*, p. 31.

33. See Linson, pp. 55–56.

34. Beer, p. 119.

35. Garland to Crane, April 17, 1894, *Letters*, p. 35.

36. Crane to Garland, April 18, 1894, *ibid.*, p. 35. Stallman mistakenly redates this letter April 17 (it is dated April 18 by Crane) on the grounds that Crane wrote Garland first. But it is clear from the contents of Crane's letter that he is replying to Garland's inquiry of the 17th concerning "how things are going with you" and that the letter is therefore correctly dated "Wednesday" by Crane (i.e., the 18th).

37. Garland to Crane, April 22, 1894, *ibid.*, p. 36. Franklin Garland was still playing in Herne's *Shore Acres* at Daly's Theatre. Herne was also producing a revival of his radical play *Margaret Fleming* at the Fifth

Avenue Theatre, where it ran from April 9 to April 28.

38. Garland to Crane, May 8, 1894, *ibid.*, p. 36.

39. Crane to Garland, November 15, 1894, *ibid.*, p. 41. This still leaves unsolved the undated letter to "Dicon" (the journalist John Henry Dick) in which Crane also asks for $15 to rescue his war story from a typist. The letter is dated "late February, 1894" by Stallman, who also indicates that *The Red Badge* was intended at that time for McClure. Since Crane had *The Red Badge* typed for McClure in April, 1894, the Dicon letter probably involves a second attempt by Crane to borrow $15 in April, 1894, or an attempt involving an unknown publisher at an unknown date. There is no evidence to support Stallman's belief that Garland lent Crane $30 in all—$15 to reclaim *The Red Badge* and another $15 to repay Dicon. The image of the two armies facing each other like animals across a river, which Garland admired in the opening lines of the typescript, was probably revised in the holograph manuscript that served as the basis for the printed version of *The Red Badge*.

40. Letter, Garland to Herbert S. Stone, postmarked April 26, 1894, in the Yale University Library.

41. Crane never tired of stating his gratitude to Garland. He dedicated *The Black Riders* (1895) to Garland and named him one of his literary executors before his trip to Cuba as a war correspondent. See also *Letters*, pp. 95, 109; *Roadside Meetings*, pp. 204–5; Linson, pp. 82–83; and Linson to Garland, January 26, 1926, in the University of Southern California Library. In his letter Linson wrote: "I am certain, Mr. Garland, that you and Howells had more to do with the vitality of his morale in those days than any others whomsoever."

12—Stephen Crane's *Maggie* and American Naturalism

1. The interpretation of *Maggie* which follows has been evolving in criticism of the novel for some years, though it has not been pursued as fully or pointedly as I do here. Both R. W. Stallman, in "Crane's *Maggie*: A

Reassessment," *Modern Fiction Studies*, V (Autumn, 1959), 251–59, and Charles C. Walcutt, in *American Literary Naturalism, A Divided Stream* (Minneapolis, 1956), pp. 67–72, touch briefly on the them of *Maggie* somewhat as I do. I have also been aided by Edwin H. Cady, *Stephen Crane* (New York, 1962), pp. 102–11; Joseph X. Brennan, "Ironic and Symbolic Structure in Crane's *Maggie*," *Nineteenth-Century Fiction*, XVI (March, 1962), 303–15; and Janet Overmyer. "The Structure of Crane's *Maggie*," *University of Kansas City Review*, XXIX (Autumn, 1962), 71–72.

2. Stephen Crane, *The Red Badge of Courage and Selected Prose and Poetry*, ed. William M. Gibson (New York, 1956), p. 1. References will hereafter appear in the text.

3. *Stephen Crane: Letters*, ed. R. W. Stallman and Lillian Gilkes (New York, 1960), p. 14.

13 – Synthetic Criticism and Frank Norris's *The Octopus*

1. *Massachusetts Review*, I (October, 1959), 62–95. This essay appears in somewhat revised form in Professor Marx's *The Machine in the Garden* (New York, 1964).

2. My italics.

3. *The Economic Novel in America* (Chapel Hill, 1942), p. 325.

4. The first two paragraphs of the following discussion of *The Octopus* summarize the thesis of my "The Concept of Nature in Frank Norris' *The Octopus*," *American Quarterly*, XIV (Spring, 1962), 73–80.

5. *The Complete Edition of Frank Norris* (Garden City, N. Y., 1928), II, 343. Citations hereafter appear in the text.

6. This theme is even more explicit in *The Pit*, where the two opposing groups (the bulls and the bears) are similar, despite their antagonism, because both use the need for wheat as a means of speculative gain. *The Pit* also contains a more elaborate and simplified discussion of the omnipotence of the law of supply and demand in

determining the production of wheat, an idea dramatized in *The Octopus* but introduced explicitly only briefly by Shelgrim. These few remarks of Shelgrim's, all of which derive from his idea that " 'Where there is a demand sooner or later there will be a supply' " (II, 285), have caused much anguish among readers of the novel, since Presley appears to be wholly convinced by Shelgrim's defense of the railroad as but " 'a force born out of certain conditions.' " What such readers fail to recognize is that within the context of the novel Shelgrim's use of the law of supply and demand as a defense of the railroad's practices is contravened in two major ways. First, the punishment of Behrman suggests that men are responsible for evil acts committed while participating in the fulfillment of natural laws. Secondly, Cedarquist's call for an aroused public to curb the excesses of the trust implies that such acts can be controlled to permit natural laws to operate more efficiently and with greater benefit. Norris, in other words, attributes to the railroad a conventional defense of its malpractices in order to demonstrate the falsity of that defense. Although Norris would accept Shelgrim's argument that the railroad and the farmer are inevitable forces which have risen to play necessary roles in the functioning of the law of supply and demand, he would deny Shelgrim's plea that individual railroads and individual farmers are not responsible for the ways in which they perform their roles. Presley is taken in by Shelgrim's defense because he has an incomplete awareness at this point of the relationship of individuals to moral law.

7. Lois Whitney, *Primitivism and the Idea of Progress in English Popular Literature of the Eighteenth Century* (Baltimore, 1934).

BIBLIOGRAPHY

The following list is restricted to specialized studies of late nineteenth-century American intellectual and literary history, and to general studies of realism and naturalism which are relevant to late nineteenth-century American literature. It omits most standard surveys of American literature, fiction, and criticism, and criticism of individual authors and works. Many of the latter are referred to in the notes.

BOOKS AND PARTS OF BOOKS

Ahnebrink, Lars. *The Beginnings of Naturalism in American Fiction.* Cambridge, Mass., 1950.

Auerbach, Erich. *Mimesis: The Representation of Reality in Western Literature.* Princeton, 1953.

Becker, George J. "Modern Realism as a Literary Movement," *Documents of Modern Literary Realism,* ed. George J. Becker. Princeton, 1963.

Booth, Wayne C. *The Rhetoric of Fiction.* Chicago, 1961.

Bowers, David F. "Hegel, Darwin, and the American Tradition," *Foreign Influences in American Life,* ed. David F. Bowers. Princeton, 1944.

Brooks, Van Wyck. *The Confident Years: 1885–1915.* New York, 1952.

Cargill, Oscar. *Intellectual America: Ideas on the March.* New York, 1941.

Carter, Everett. *Howells and the Age of Realism.* Philadelphia, 1954.

Chase, Richard. *The American Novel and Its Tradition*. Garden City, N. Y., 1957.

Cowley, Malcolm. "Naturalism in American Literature," *Evolutionary Thought in America*, ed. Stow Persons. New Haven, 1950.

Falk, Robert P. "The Rise of Realism, 1871–1891," *Transitions in American Literary History*, ed. Harry H. Clark. Durham, N. C., 1953.

———. "The Literary Criticism of the Genteel Decades: 1870–1900," *The Development of American Literary Criticism*, ed. Floyd Stovall. Chapel Hill, 1955.

———. "The Search for Reality: Writers and Their Literature," *The Gilded Age: A Reappraisal*, ed. H. Wayne Morgan. Syracuse, 1963.

———. *The Victorian Mode in American Fiction, 1865–1885*. East Lansing, Mich., 1965.

Farrell, James T. "Some Observations on Naturalism, So Called, in Fiction," *Reflections at Fifty and Other Essays*. New York, 1954.

Geismar, Maxwell. *Rebels and Ancestors: The American Novel, 1890–1915*. Boston, 1953.

Hofstadter, Richard. *Social Darwinism in American Thought, 1860–1915*. Philadelphia, 1945.

Kahn, Sholom J. *Science and Aesthetic Judgment: A Study in Taine's Critical Method*. New York, 1953.

Kazin, Alfred. *On Native Grounds*. New York, 1942.

———. "American Naturalism: Reflections from Another Era," *The American Writer and the European Tradition*, ed. Margaret Denny and William H. Gilman. Minneapolis, 1950.

Knight, Grant C. *The Critical Period in American Literature*. Chapel Hill, 1951.

Levin, Harry. *The Gates of Horn*. New York, 1963.

Lynn, Kenneth S. *The Dream of Success*. Boston, 1955.

Munro, Thomas. *Evolution in the Arts*. New York, 1963.

Persons, Stow, ed. *Evolutionary Thought in America*. New Haven, 1950.

Rahv, Philip. "Notes on the Decline of Naturalism," *Image and Idea*. New York, 1949.

Stone, Edward, ed. *What Was Naturalism?* New York, 1959.

Taylor, Walter F. *The Economic Novel in America.* Chapel Hill, 1942.

Trilling, Lionel. "Reality in America," *The Liberal Imagination.* New York, 1950.

Walcutt, Charles C. *American Literary Naturalism, A Divided Stream.* Minneapolis, 1956.

Watt, Ian. "Realism and the Novel Form," *The Rise of the Novel.* Berkeley and Los Angeles, 1960.

Wellek, René. "The Concept of Evolution in Literary History," *Concepts of Criticism.* New Haven, 1963.

————. "The Concept of Realism in Literary Scholarship," *Concepts of Criticism.* New Haven, 1963.

ARTICLES

Bowron, Bernard R. "Realism in America," *Comparative Literature*, III (Summer, 1951), 200–17.

Carter, Everett. "The Meaning of, and in, Realism," *Antioch Review*, XIII (Spring, 1952), 78–94.

Clark, Harry H. "The Influence of Science on American Literary Criticism, 1860–1910 . . . ," *Transactions of the Wisconsin Academy of Sciences, Arts and Letters*, XLIV (1955), 109–64.

Greenwood, E. B. "Reflections on Professor Wellek's Concept of Realism," *Neophilologus*, XLVI (April, 1962), 89–97.

Jones, A. E. "Darwinism and Its Relation to Realism and Naturalism in American Fiction, 1860–1900," *Drew University Bulletin*, XXXVIII (December, 1950), 3–21.

Levin, Harry. "What is Realism?" *Comparative Literature*, III (Summer, 1951), 193–98.

Marx, Leo. "Two Kingdoms of Force," *Massachusetts Review*, I (October, 1959), 69–95.

Meyer, George W. "The Original Social Purpose of the Naturalistic Novel," *Sewanee Review*, L (October, 1942), 563–70.

Peckham, Morse. "Darwinism and Darwinisticism," *Victorian Studies*, III (September, 1959), 19–40.

Randall, John H. "The Changing Impact of Darwin on Philosophy," *Journal of the History of Ideas*, XXII (October–December, 1961), 435–62.

Wellek, René. "A Reply to E. B. Greenwood's Reflections," *Neophilologus*, XLVI (July, 1962), 194–96.

Williams, Raymond. "Realism and the Contemporary Novel," *Partisan Review*, XXVI (Spring, 1959), 200–13.

INDEX

Taine, Hippolyte A.: influence on Garland, 39, 70, 90; on Posnett, 40; on Howells, 42, 44; on Perry, 60; on criticism, 79–80

Taylor, Walter Fuller: *The Economic Novel in America,* 133–36, 143

Thoreau, Henry David, 101, 133, 134

Tolstoy, Count Leo, 65, 113

Trent, Helen, 116

Trevelyan, George M.: *English Social History,* 78

Trilling, Lionel, 20

Turgenev, Ivan, 65

Twain, Mark: realism in, 3–10; mentioned, 135

—*Adventures of Huckleberry Finn,* 3–10, 107, 134, 141

Utilitarianism, 110–13

Valdés, Armando, 93
Veritism, 93–94

Véron, Eugène: influence on Garland, 91–92

—*Aesthetics,* 91–92; *Supériorité des arts modernes sur les arts anciens, La,* 91

Walcutt, Charles C.: *American Literary Naturalism,* 145n2

Walker, Franklin, 99

Wave, 35

Whitman, Walt, 40, 94

Whitney, Lois, 140

Wilde, Oscar: and Norris, 101–3; *De Profundis,* 102

Yale Review, 114

Yellow Book, 101

Zola, Émile: and Norris, 33–36, 141; mentioned, 89, 146n7

—*L'Assommoir,* 19, 122; *Débâcle, La,* 35, 147n9; *Fécondité,* 35, 148n9; *Nana,* 122, 127; *Terre, La,* 35, 147n9